The P⸺⸺ ⸺⸺⸺

# THE MARX BROTHERS

www.pocketessentials.com

First published in Great Britain 2001 by Pocket Essentials, 18 Coleswood Road,
Harpenden, Herts, AL5 1EQ

Distributed in the USA by Trafalgar Square Publishing, PO Box 257, Howe Hill
Road, North Pomfret, Vermont 05053

Copyright © Mark Bego 2001
Series Editor: Paul Duncan

A CIP catalogue record for this book is available from the British Library.

ISBN 1-903047-59-5

1 3 5 7 9 10 8 6 4 2

Book typeset by Pdunk
Printed and bound by Cox & Wyman

*For Glenn Hughes: Millions of fans around the world knew you as the Leatherman in the Village People, but I will always remember you as a dear friend.*

## Acknowledgements

The author would like to thank Bob & Mary Bego, Paul Donnelley, Paul Duncan, Janet Dammann, Jan Kalajian, David Kelly, Ion Mills, Bobby Reed and Beth Wernick.

# CONTENTS

1. Introduction - The Brothers Marx ............................7

2. The Family Business - Show Business...................9

3. The Vaudeville Years .................................................14

4. Minnie's Boys In Chicago...............................21

5. The Road Back To Broadway............................35

6. The First Films.................................................43

7. Hooray For Hollywood ...............................51

8. The TV And Radio Years....................................80

9. Obscure Marx Films And Shorts.......................85

10. Video And DVD Guide............................................88

11. Quote Sources...................................................89

12. Bibliography ............................................91

13. Websites......................................................92

# 1. Introduction - The Brothers Marx

When you think of the classic comedies of the 1930s, it's hard not to recall the painted-on moustache and cigar smoke of Groucho Marx, the malapropism-ladened Italian accent of Chico Marx, the pantomime harp-playing clown Harpo Marx or the bumbling straight man as characterised by Zeppo Marx. They were The Marx Brothers and together they produced some of the most memorable, joke-filled, hysterical movies and comedy moments ever filmed.

This family of brothers, whose impressive body of work includes *Duck Soup*, *Horse Feathers*, *Animal Crackers*, *A Night At The Opera* and *A Night In Casablanca*, performed with each other for five decades. There was never a comic troupe quite like The Marx Brothers, although their antics inspired countless comedians including: The Three Stooges, Abbott and Costello, Dean Martin and Jerry Lewis, and even Cheech & Chong.

However, The Marx Brothers were not a product of Hollywood at all. For 20 years before they set foot on a movie soundstage, they struggled on the vaudeville circuit, playing in every town and whistle-stop in the United States and Canada. Their mother Minnie Marx was part of the act, was their manager and was often their producer. There was even a fifth brother, Gummo, who dropped out of the act before fame finally struck.

Finally, after years of struggling, The Marx Brothers arrived when *I'll Say She Is* became the surprise Broadway hit of 1924. Suddenly they were on a hot streak. They quickly followed it with *The Cocoanuts*, which ran from October 1925 to November 1927, and then *Animal Crackers* in October 1928.

In 1929, when motion pictures with sound were suddenly all the rage and set to revolutionise the film business, studios were

7

scrambling to find actors who could not only act, but who could sing and talk as well. They looked to Broadway and so The Marx Brothers made *The Cocoanuts* in 1929. It was the first of 13 full-length feature films they made in a 20-year span. The rest, as they say, is history.

Thanks to video, and now DVDs, the films of The Marx Brothers are still very much alive and accessible to modern audiences. Hopefully this book will inspire you to investigate the classic comedy work of The Marx Brothers, or perhaps discover a forgotten classic or two that you have never had the opportunity to see before.

The films are rated as follows:

    1/5 – OK, with fun moments

    2/5 - Amusing

    3/5 – Very Good

    4/5 – Great

    5/5 - Classic

# 2. The Family Business - Show Business

To fully appreciate The Marx Brothers story, one has to go all the way back into their past to see how their individual characters, and their entire act, evolved. Groucho, Chico, Harpo, Gummo and Zeppo each owe as much credit to their family roots in show business, as they do in their own vast talent as comedians, musicians and actors.

The Schönberg family came from the area of Germany then known as Prussia. They moved in the late 1800s to New York City. At the time, Meine (Minnie) Schönberg was fifteen years old. It was in New York City that she met Samuel ("Frenchy") Marx, formerly of Alsace, France. They fell in love and were married January 18, 1885.

Samuel and Minnie Marx and their large family lived on Manhattan's Upper East Side, in an area known as Yorkville, which was a neighbourhood teaming with German immigrants. The Marx clan resided at 197 East 93rd Street. As Groucho was to later recall, 'In addition to the five brothers...there were my father and mother (in fact they got there before we did), my mother's father and mother, an adopted sister and a steady stream of poor relations that flowed through our house night and day.' (1) (See Chapter 11 for Quote Source 1) The adopted sister was actually the boys' cousin Pauline, or "Polly" as she was nicknamed.

Minnie's brother was Al Shean (1868-1948) who became famous as one half of the vaudeville duo: Gallagher & Shean. Al Shean was to be instrumental in the growing stardom of his young nephews, before finding fame of his own in the *Ziegfeld Follies Of 1922* on Broadway. The big number that was to make them household names was called 'Oh Mr Gallagher, Oh Mr Shean.'

The Marx boys' maternal grandparents, Levy Schönberg (1823-1920) and his wife, Fanny Sophie Solomons Schönberg (1829-1901), had show-business roots themselves. However, when they arrived in America, their career on the stage came to a crashing end - the victim of moving to a new country where German was rarely spoken outside of the neighbourhood. As Groucho explained, 'Since neither my grandfather nor my grandmother spoke any English, they were unable to get any theatrical dates in America. For some curious reason there seemed to be practically no demand for a German ventriloquist and a woman harpist who yodelled in a foreign language.' (1) However, no one suspected how instrumental that very harp was to be in later shaping the career of one particular member of The Marx Brothers.

Prior to finding success with Gallagher, Uncle Al Shean performed with several partners in a variety of acts, including The Manhattan Quartet (1894) and The Manhattan Comedy Four. By 1899 Al was not only a featured singer and comedian, but he also graduated to become a writer of his own stage material. His trademark style became a series of wisecracking malapropisms and comically confused one-liners. This same silly stage banter was to become the staple of The Marx Brothers' routines in later years - especially between Groucho and Chico. Al was to become very influential in the development of the boys' act as a performing troupe - as a role model and as a writer.

Just after the turn of the century, Uncle Al Shean was appearing with a new partner, Charles Warren. They performed different comedy skits including 'Quo Vadis Upside Down' (1901) and 'Kidding The Captain,' which was a spoof of 'Captain Kidd.' Adept at penning witty satire, it was Uncle Al Shean who was to write one of The Marx Brothers' first hit shows, *Home*

*Again*, which ran from 1914 to 1918. But, we are getting ahead of ourselves here!

Minnie (Miene) and Samuel (Simon) Marx had six boys. The first one, Manfred, was born in January 1896, and sadly died in July of that year. Their other sons were: Leonard (Leo/Chico) Marx, born March 22, 1887; Adolph (Arthur/Harpo) Marx, born November 21, 1888; Julius Henry (Groucho) Marx, born October 2, 1890; Milton (Gummo) Marx, born October 23, 1892; and Herbert (Zeppo) Marx, born February 25, 1901.

The boys' father, whose nickname was Frenchy, due to his dapper appearance, floated from career to career over the years. Eventually the boys supported the family, with Mama Minnie becoming their manager. Frenchy had one unsuccessful business venture after another, including one stint as a tailor. Unfortunately, according to his sons, he was the worst tailor anyone could imagine. Eventually, Frenchy found out that he was great in the kitchen and he became the family cook. According to Groucho, no one could cook quite like Frenchy could.

The three oldest boys had very strong personalities from the very start. Because Leonard (Chico) had been born and - unlike Manfred - survived, he grew up being the favourite, or the favoured son. Leonard always felt that he was loved and cared for, and Minnie spoiled him. He had a cocky sense of self-confidence, and he learned to hustle cards or dice at a very early age. By the time he was 12 years old, he was already a compulsive gambler.

Adolph (Harpo) was known in the family as 'the good son.' He became a mimic at an early age. Every day after school he would pass a cigar store, and watch a man in the window rolling cigars and making a cross-eyed, round-mouthed, tongue-rolled face while he did so. Adolph copied this look, which he called his "gookie" face, and it was to become one of his trademark bits as a comedian.

Julius was the intellectual son. He loved to read so much that he would sometimes lock himself in the family bathroom with a book so that he wouldn't be disturbed. His grasp of knowledge, both of facts and of words, made him the blossoming intellectual the world would come to know as "Groucho." He was always good with his money from an early age.

One of the most confusing factors of telling the story of The Marx Brothers, is the fact that Minnie had a habit of lying about her sons' ages. Up to five years was added or subtracted for many assumed reasons. One of the first reasons for this deception was to make certain that Minnie's boys successfully avoided being drafted into American military service. The family didn't escape from Europe only to lose its sons in the brewing European conflict which would eventually blossom into World War I. The second convenient birth date deception was a show business-based one. When each of the boys wandered onto the stage, they did so playing juvenile or youth roles. How much more talented a child would look on stage if he claimed to be only 14, when he was in fact a semi-adult 19-year-old. In the ensuing years, there were apparently several reported incidents in which young teenage Groucho would be caught in front of a theatre's men's room mirror, shaving off all of the evidence of a more mature man's five o'clock shadow.

From an early age - around 11, Minnie's oldest son Chico had a keen sense of street smarts, hanging out with tough street gangs and staying out until all hours of the night. By the time he was 12, Chico had dropped out of school and was working for a lace factory, where his job was to keep track of the other employees' hours. As luck, or misfortune, was to have it, there was a revolving crap game at the factory, and when it was discovered that Chico was gambling on the premises - he was fired.

To keep their eldest son off the streets, Minnie and Frenchy bought a used piano and hired a music teacher for him. Both piano playing and gambling were to become lifelong passions for Chico.

13

# 3. The Vaudeville Years

The Marx boys wandered into the world of show business in various ways. The first Marx brother to enter showbiz was Chico. In fact, he was employed in the movies! Not on screen however. His first film career was as a piano player in silent-film theatres and nickelodeons. Later he graduated to playing piano in saloons and dance halls as well.

The first of Minnie's boys to actually perform on stage was Milton (Gummo). Apparently, Uncle Heinie (Henry/Harry), Uncle Al Shean's brother, figured that if Al could make a living in show business, so could he, and he decided to use Grandpa Levy Schönberg's ventriloquism act. The fact that Uncle Heinie had zero talent as a ventriloquist wasn't about to throw a wrench in his plans either. The idea he struck upon was to use a hollow dummy's head, put Milton inside the little outfit and pass him off as a supposedly mute mannequin. The far-fetched charade called for Heinie mid-act to stab the dummy's leg with a long pin to prove that it was in fact an inanimate dummy in the costume, and not a real live person. The deception called for both of little Milton's legs to be shoved into one pant leg of the dummy's costume, while the other one was to be stuffed. However, when it was time for the revealing hat-pin ploy to take place on stage, forgetful Heinie stabbed Milton in the wrong leg, and the child leapt from his uncle's leg, writhing in pain. Needless to say - this was to be a very short-lived act.

Groucho was later to recall that he was then cast as Heinie's dummy for a short time. 'I did an act with my uncle, Harry Shean. The fact that he was completely deaf didn't make a difference...We concocted an act which consisted of a ventriloquist's dummy, in which I was inside. The head was over my head, and I operated the mechanical part as well as speaking.

Uncle Henry just stood there. That the act lasted only a couple of weeks is evidence that it was not a success.' (2)

Speaking of his own entry into show business, Groucho explained, 'The first real job I ever got was on Coney Island. I sang a song on a beer keg and made a dollar. Later I sang in a Protestant church choir, until they found out what was wrong with it. For that I got a dollar every Sunday... I began my show-business career at the age of 15, in 1905, by answering a classified ad in *The New York Morning World*. The job called for a boy singer for a vaudeville act, room and board and four dollars a week. When I saw the ad, I ran all the way from our house on 93rd Street to 33rd Street. The man's name was Leroy and I looked for his name on the mailbox. Then I ran up five flights of stairs and knocked on the door. A man answered. He was in a kimono and wearing lipstick. This was the profession I wanted to get into?' (3)

Groucho landed the job. However, the act's first engagement was in far-off Colorado, and both he and Leroy were performing in drag. When that act flopped, young Groucho found himself stranded in Colorado, hundreds and hundreds of miles away from New York City. He had to support himself by delivering groceries until Minnie could wire enough money to him for train fare back home.

When Groucho got back to Manhattan, his mother was so impressed by his moxie that she decided to become his personal career manager. The first job she landed him was as a singer in a beer garden. Networking her way into the show-business world, she became acquainted with Lily Seville, who was searching for a juvenile singer for her act. And so began Groucho's career in vaudeville as one half of the attraction which was billed as Lily Seville And Master Marx.

The first newspaper mention of him came from *The Dallas Morning News*, December 25, 1905, which reported, 'Master Marx is a boy tenor, who introduces bits of Jewish character from the East Side of New York. The act is a novelty and will be appreciated by the Majestic audience.' (4)

Less than a fortnight later, a reviewer in *The San Antonio Light* claimed that Lily and Julius' act was 'very high class as a study of human types... She sings several coster ballads and is assisted in the act by Master Marx, a juvenile soprano singer and impersonator of the Yiddischer.' (5)

After that act ran its gamut, it was back to Manhattan for Master Marx. Having returned to the home nest, the next act Minnie steered Groucho into was as one of Gus Edwards' Postal Telegraph Boys. The act opened on April 28, 1906, at the Alhambra Theater.

Coincidentally, the biggest natural disaster of the new century had occurred ten days before. On April 18, the San Francisco earthquake and the subsequent out-of-control fires it caused all but levelled the entire city. New York City rallied almost instantly to come to the aid of the countless victims. To offer support, Gus Edwards had his Postal Telegraph Boys performing at several chic Broadway restaurants to sing and solicit cash donations towards the relief fund. Young Groucho sang at such establishments as the Café Des Beaux Arts, Café Martin and Churchill's Restaurant.

On Friday, May 3, 1906, Gus Edwards' Postal Telegraph Boys were in a huge benefit held at the Metropolitan Opera House as part of a gala San Francisco earthquake charity effort. Also on the bill that night were such Broadway and international stars as Ethel Barrymore and Lillian Russell. Groucho was later to recall, 'I went on stage with a 70-piece orchestra and sang 'Somebody's Sweetheart I Want To Be.'' (3)

For proud Jewish mama, Minnie Marx, it was an inspiring moment. She never dreamed that she would have her son Julius singing at the prestigious Metropolitan Opera House before a crowd of 3,000 people. The event fuelled her imagination towards what kind of achievements were truly possible.

The Postal Telegraph Boys was an act which was a revolving door for young singers. By August 1906, Groucho had already moved on and was featured in a legitimate play called *A Man Of Her Choice*, in which he portrayed the role of Jimmy, The Office Boy.

Meanwhile, Harpo was working as a piano player in a whorehouse in Freeport, Long Island. Around this time, Chico was bouncing from job to job - including packing blotting paper in a factory. However, even at this young phase of his professional life, he usually gambled away most of his earnings.

In the spring of 1907, Groucho and Gummo entered into a vaudeville apprenticeship of one Ned Wayburn, at 143 West 44th Street. Also under Wayburn's tutelage at the same time was a singer named Mabel O'Donell, and a dancing duo calling themselves The Astaire Children. They were eight-year-old Fred and his ten-year-old sister Adele.

It was Ned's intention to feature Mabel in his revue as the lead singer in a group to be called Wayburn's Nightingales. With Groucho and Gummo Marx as the other two Nightingales, the Marx boys were clad in little sailor suits which Mama Minnie found on sale at Bloomingdale's Department Store.

By mid-1907, Minnie Marx had swept in to begin managing The Nightingales. With Ned Wayburn's publicity machinery, and top theatrical bookings, The Nightingales were gaining popularity. In the November 30, 1906 issue of *Variety*, they were heralded for one such appearance with the billing: 'The Three Nightingales, big hit Everywhere - Minnie Marx, manager.' (6)

And so was born the saga of one of the most famous stage mothers in show-business history. She was eclipsed in this honour only by Gypsy Rose Lee's indomitable Mama Rose. Interestingly enough, both of these famed vaudeville mothers were canonised by having Broadway shows named after them. Rose, of course, is known for having the hit musical *Gypsy* to tell her story. Minnie Marx and her sons were to be portrayed in a Broadway musical of their own - *Minnie's Boys*, which ran in New York City in 1970. The play starred Shelley Winters as Minnie Marx.

In an article in *Liberty* magazine in 1933, writer Clara Beranger explained, 'How those [Marx] boys love to talk about her! If you say 'your mother' to any of them, you are immediately deluged with paeans of praise and a flood of anecdotes to prove that she was not only the most remarkable woman that ever lived, but the best mother. They give her full credit for making them 'what they are today.' For teaching them to act, to sing, to clown. For helping them write their stuff and booking it with managers. For going with them on the road, selling them to any manager who had a vaudeville house and would give her brood a chance. She stayed by them, settling their disputes, arranging their financial affairs, scolding, browbeating, directing but not restraining their crazy irresponsibility on and off the stage.' (7)

Step by step, engagement by engagement, The Three Nightingales plodded along, gaining fame, and an audience for their vocal skills. According to a review in *Variety* newspaper, dated December 21, 1907, 'The larger of the youths [Groucho] does not announce the 'Dutch' imitations as formerly, though he sings one song with a distinct German dialect. The three children have splendid voices that blend beautifully... The white costumes worn at the opening should be sent to the cleaners.' (8)

In January 1908 Ned Wayburn filed for bankruptcy, leaving The Three Nightingales' future in Minnie's hands. While The

Three Nightingales were part of Ned Wayburn's act, they were featured at many of Manhattan's top theatres and clubs. With Minnie now at the reins it was back to ground zero. One of Minnie's first chores was to get Mabel out of the picture.

Minnie decided that managing a girl singer was too big a bother to tackle, so she fired Mabel and hired a fresh-faced boy named Lou Levy. Groucho was later to recall, 'We played some pretty good theatres because basically Mabel O'Donnell was a pretty good singer in spite of the fact that she was cockeyed. Her big problem was she always went off key. That's why we finally had to let her go and ended up getting some boy to take her place.' (2)

Groucho later wrote, 'I can never look at a fish without thinking of that cheerless week in Atlantic City when The Three Nightingales were singing in the Atlantic City Garden. The salary for the act was 40 dollars a week - with board. And, while the board was certainly plentiful, it consisted of nothing but fish. That wasn't because the theatre manager - he also owned the boarding house - regarded fish as brain food and healthful. He happened to keep a huge fish net right below my bedroom window, and at night I could hear my breakfast, lunch and dinner swimming into the net.' (9)

Minnie's next matter of business was to turn The Three Nightingales to The Four Nightingales. What had happened was that Minnie had cut a deal with the United Booking Office to take over scheduling the act at several major theatres across the country. However, the United Booking Office insisted that they required a quartet, and not a trio. Suddenly Harpo Marx, who never considered himself a singer, was going to become a professional singer.

According to Harpo, 'While I was working at the nickelodeon... one afternoon, in the middle of the movie, my mother marched down the aisle of the theatre to the piano. She ordered me to leave at once and come with her. Minnie's face was set with desperation and determination. She was in some kind of a jam, and from the look of her, it could be serious trouble. Minnie had never come to me for help in a crisis before.' (10)

Groucho was to add that Minnie was to insist, '"Instead of calling the act The Three Nightingales, we'll call it The Four Nightingales! It's a great name! I'll go over to Bloomingdale's this afternoon and get two more white outfits. And you, [Adolph]," she added, "while I'm gone, you practise singing bass."'

When Harpo argued that he couldn't sing, she insisted, "Keep your mouth open and no one will know the difference." (1)

Harpo later recalled that he was so terrified at the prospect of having to sing on stage that the first time he performed as the fourth Nightingale he literally peed his pants with fright. But, pants wet with urine or not, he sang. He learned his part of the four-part harmony act and on the road he went.

# 4. Minnie's Boys In Chicago

By August 14, 1909, the act had further evolved, and even Mama Minnie had joined the stage show - in the comedy segments. It was now billed as Minnie Marx And Her Four Nightingales.

Instead of employing other performers when additional roles need to be filled, the whole family - even Minnie's sister, the boys' Aunt Hannah - got roped into the act. With Hannah aboard for the hi-jinx, the act evolved into a new show called The Six Mascots. The cast of The Six Mascots included Groucho, Harpo, Gummo, Lou Levy, Minnie and Aunt Hannah Schönberg.

To make a fresh start for her family troupe, Minnie moved the clan to Chicago and took a new professional name: Minnie Palmer. The fact that the name already belonged to a noted singer of the late 1800s was not wasted on Mrs Marx. In fact, she relished the confusion. Since the real Minnie Palmer had long since married and moved to England, many fans of the original owner of the name confused her for the original. For Mama Marx, this only added to her clout in negotiating contracts, and gave her assumed power, scope and appeal. Around this same time, Lou Levy was replaced in the act by a new Nightingale, Freddie Hutchins.

By now, there were only two things missing from the act: Zeppo and Chico. Zeppo was only seven years old in 1908, so he had to wait his turn to join the family on stage. But, what of older brother Chico? From 1908 to 1910, he was involved in several different ventures. For a time he moved from New York City to Pittsburgh, Pennsylvania, where he worked for a music publishing house called Shapiro, Bernstein & Company. However there was - as the old circus/showbiz adage goes - still sawdust running through his veins. With teenage friend Arthur Gordon, Chico started a new act. Having become adept at imitating the Italian accent of his barber, Chico and Arthur decided to lampoon Italian immigrants in their act, Gordoni & Marx.

The act the duo put together paid their bills, and what was left over Chico gambled away. Even at the early age of 21, an unfortunate pattern had been set: whatever extra money Chico was to earn in his life was soon gambled away on the roll of dice, a game of cards or a horse-race bet.

After the Gordoni & Marx routine ran its course, Chico attempted a solo vaudeville act but with little success. In 1911, he joined his Uncle Al Shean and they performed as a duo. According to a review in the October 7, 1911 issue of *Variety*, the act was well received. 'Shean and Marx are quite new and... good,' claimed the reviewer who wrote under the singular name of Wynn. 'Marx is an exceptionally good piano player with a certain personality that stands out, while Shean can warble with the best.' (11) Unfortunately, the act was short lived. Eventually, Al and Chico migrated to Chicago as well, to become part of the growing family enterprise. At the time, Chicago was second only to New York City as the capitol of the vaudeville world. It was also to become the launching pad for the act that the world came to know as The Marx Brothers. When Al and Chico both reached the Windy City, they found that Minnie Palmer had parts for both of them in her latest show-business scheme.

Circa 1911, the family's act was billed as The Three Marx Brothers, and it consisted of Groucho, Gummo and Harpo. Still finding their stage personas, it was Groucho - not Harpo - who was in the red fright wig, acting like a clown. To round out the act and turn it into an appealing musical revue, Minnie included an ever-changing group of chorus girls in the troupe to add sex appeal to the act, and to draw in an avid male audience of theatre patrons.

The musical segment of the show consisted of Groucho playing the featured piano parts, and Harpo doing his now-famous harp solos mid-show. The act was set in a school classroom, with Groucho as the Dutch-accented teacher and Harpo as the incredibly dense Irish character, Patsy Brannigan. The Marx Brothers' first attempts at a 'school act' was one which had a revolving cast of characters brought together in a rural multi-ethnic school. Mama Minnie and Aunt Hannah portrayed the bewildered and not-so-bright schoolgirls.

At the time there was another popular classroom act on the vaudeville circuit called Gus Edwards' School Boys And Girls. The February 24, 1912 issue of *Variety* reviewed the antics of the Marx family's stage act, and pointed out, 'When Gus Edwards' School Boys And Girls recently appeared at Hammerstein's, it was mentioned in a criticism in this paper that there were 'school acts' on the 'small time' much better than Mr Edwards' played-out turn. The act arrived sooner than expected. It is The Marx Brothers, from the west.' (11)

It is interesting to note that bits and pieces of The Marx Brothers' classic routines were constantly being recycled and retooled for future projects. The tone and flavour of the brothers' school act can today be spotted on film in *Horse Feathers*, where Groucho is seen reprising his long-running post as the frustrated schoolteacher, instructing a classroom of idiots.

As far back as 1912, the ploy of having Harpo play his grandmother's harp was one of the most winning aspects of their stage show. The unique musical interlude was so successful, in fact, that around this same era, the decision was made to splurge and spend the astronomical sum of $54 on a brand new harp for Harpo to play.

In 1912, Chico and Uncle Al Shean dissolved their duet act, while Groucho, Harpo and Gummo were touring in their hit classroom act, *Fun In Hi Skule*. According to an article in *Variety* dated May 19, 1912, 'Shean and Marx have separated as a vaudeville team and Leonard Marx, who played the piano in the former offering, has doubled with George Lee, ex-comedian with 'The Arlington Four.' Marx occasionally writes a song hit and incidentally is one of the several children of Minnie Palmer, who is represented in vaudeville with several acts, among them being The Marx Brothers, a 'school act' made up practically of one family.' (12)

In the summer of that year, the school act was retooled slightly as the play *Mr Green's Reception* and featured four Marx brothers in it. This version of the show was divided into three acts. It included the same tried and true classroom act, with Groucho as the Dutch teacher, and the later part of the show took place ten years later, in which the teacher, Mr Green, gives a party for his old pupils.

As described in the January 13, 1913 *Kalamazoo Gazette*, it was about 'the smart doings and sayings of his precocious pupils of who, there are a dozen or more, mostly pretty girls, with short skirts, yellow hair and pink stockings... *Mr Green's Reception* is in three acts and is described as a 'modern mixture of mirth, melody and motion.' In it are an unusually large number of tuneful melodies, the principal ones of which are 'When I Met You Last Night,' 'Circus Day,' 'Roll Me Around Like A Hoop, My Dear,' 'Yittsky College Boy,' 'Days Of Boys And Girls,' 'Hello Mr Stein,' 'Beautiful Nights, Beautiful Girls,' 'Robert E Lee,' and other tuneful triumphs.' (13)

One of the routines has found Groucho as Mr Green, lamenting: "Nowadays you don't know how much you know until your children grow up and tell you how much you don't know." Another segment has Chico as Leo The Wop announcing to Mr Green, "I'd like-a to say goodbye to your wife." To which, Groucho's Mr Green replies: "Who wouldn't?" Clearly, the banter that made The Marx Brothers famous was already well in place in 1913 when *Mr Green's Reception* debuted.

The mixture of pretty girls and songs bridging The Marx Brothers' comedy bits was one which would define their act for quite some time. It is interesting to note that the singing and dancing segments were responsible for keeping Gummo interested in remaining as part of the act throughout this era. Possessing a speech impediment and the habit of stuttering when he was nervous, the song and dance segments masked his insecurity from the audience.

In addition to being the producer of her sons' touring act, Minnie Palmer also had other features on the road as well. They included The Dukes Of Durham and The Seven Orange Blossoms. She also managed a troupe of chorines who were called Minnie Palmer's Parisian Violets.

Touring the United States and Canada on the Pantages Theatre circuit, the family act - now known as The Four Marx Brothers - was working quite steadily. Touring from town to town with *Mr Green's Reception*, the brothers Marx zigzagged back and forth across the countryside.

According to a review in the November 13, 1913 issue of *The Salt Lake Telegraph*, 'among the boy scholars are a Hebrew, an Italian, an Irishman, a German and couple of sissies.' (14)

Regarding the ethnic make-up of the act, The Marx Brothers' show was one which could appeal to a mixed-up goulash of an immigrant stew. According to Groucho, 'The frock coat was borrowed from Uncle Julius (Sthickler), and the German accent... was borrowed from [Grandpa] Opie [Schönberg]. Gummo... played a young Hebrew boy... We Marx Brothers never denied our Jewishness. We simply didn't use it. We could have safely fallen back on the Yiddish theatre, making secure careers for ourselves. But our act was designed from the start to have a broad appeal. If, because of Chico, a segment of the audience thought we were Italian, then let them.' (3)

Although they were working steadily, things weren't always rosy. Groucho Marx was later to recall, '...when I think of *Mr Green's Reception*, I think of that mournful afternoon in Battle Creek, Michigan, when we gave our entire show with only four patrons in the audience, in a theatre that seated close to 3,000.' (9)

Whenever she was interviewed in the press, Mama Minnie would promise that it wouldn't be long before her teenage son Zeppo would soon be joining the act. According to an item in a 1914 issue of the *Clipper* newspaper, 'Herbert Marx, youngest of The Marx Brothers, will change the title of the act from The Four Marx Brothers to The Five Marx Brothers as soon as he completes school. He appeared at the Willard [theatre] one night recently, and scored... big.' (15)

Zeppo Marx was later to recall, 'My mother was always trying to get the boys - Gummo, Groucho, Chico and Harpo - jobs, playing vaudeville. Cheap vaudeville, really, four or five shows a day and maybe three days' work, and then get laid off for a week or two or something. She was always downtown where the theatrical district was, where the agents and the managers were hanging out, so she would always try to get us bookings. If some act was cancelled some place, she'd try to shove us in there.' (16)

Although they were a top attraction between the two coasts, it was Broadway and Hollywood they longed to conquer, and they were still years away from accomplishing either of these goals. In 1914, it was time for the Marx family troupe to have a new vehicle in which to perform and show off their comic and musical talents. This is where Uncle Al Shean was roped into the scenario - as a playwright.

The show Al penned for his nephews was called *Home Again*, and it was almost instantly a hit. To help sell the act to theatres, Minnie took out an ad in *Variety*, guaranteeing the hit power of The Four Marx Brothers in their 38-minute, 17-person act *Home Again*. In the ad she did something that had never been done before - she guaranteed to raise any theatre's box-office grosses for any Marx Brothers engagement, or they didn't have to pay her. The ad read: 'Have the records for the Interstate Circuit at Ft. Worth and Dallas. For the first time in its history, The Majestic, Ft. Worth (week Sept. 28), had the SRO sign out for the Saturday matinee, making full capacity every performance with *Home Again* the featured attraction. Last week at the Majestic, Dallas, took all box-office records... This act is famed as a moneymaker for the house... It's got to draw, to earn its salary, and it does draw, hence the guarantee... The greatest comedy act in show business, bar none. Management, Minnie Palmer.' (17)

When *Home Again* opened at the Lincoln Hippodrome in Chicago, the reviewer loved what he saw. According to the review published in *Variety*, 'This merry little musical short gives The Four Marx Bros. opportunity to do some very effective work in their several lines. They all have talent, and they shine in this piece which allows them time to display their own brand of rollicking humour in which they excel... The story concerns Henry Schneider (Julius Marx) who is returning with his family and friends from a voyage across the ocean... Milton Marx is seen as Harold Schneider whose chief work is to look handsome, which he does without question. Leonard Marx is seen in an Italian character, and his speciality at the piano, in which he does comic things with his hands and fingers, is one of the best features... Arthur Marx is billed as a 'nondescript.' He is made up as a 'boob' and his make-up is not pleasant. He gets a good many laughs but a change should be made in his character. He plays the harp well, and does some comedy with the strings that is in a class by itself.' (18)

Indeed, all of The Marx Brothers' individual characters were developing very strongly at this time. Groucho was honing his skills at the cynical comic star. Chico had his Italian accent down, as well as his unique piano skills. Harpo was well on his way to making his harp antics his trademark. And Gummo was paving the way for the fourth Marx brother to be the handsome straight man - a role within the act that Zeppo would soon inherit.

One of biggest evolutions to happen in the act during this era was the decision to make harp-playing Harpo into a mute or silent character. According to legend, part of the decision came during an obscure booking in the hinterlands of rural America. It seems that Groucho was caught smoking a cigar backstage, and the manager of the theatre decided to fine him $10 for his infraction to the rules. To protest this fine, The Marx Brothers refused to go on stage at the last minute unless the fine was lifted. The manager found himself over a barrel - in negotiating terms - and so reluctantly agreed. However, the theatre manager had the last laugh. When the brothers' week at the theatre was completed, they were paid their entire gross of $112.50 in copper pennies. According to Groucho, 'We barely made the train, and as it pulled out of the depot, we stood on the back platform watching the town and theatre recede into the distance. Then Harpo, the pantomimist, raised his voice, and above the clatter of the train, bellowed: 'Goodbye, Mr Wells. Here's hoping your lousy theatre burns down!' We thought it was just a gag, till the next morning - when we discovered that during the night, Jack Wells' theatre had been reduced to ashes. From then on we decided not to let Harpo talk - his conversation was too dangerous!' (19)

The play *Home Again*, was to serve The Four Marx Brothers well. In fact it did so well for them that they were to tour with it from 1914 to 1918. For one week in 1915 they even took it to the Palace Theatre on Broadway.

While the Marx family of comedians was finally hitting their stride while defining roles that would last them a lifetime, current events in the world were taking place which would shape the future as well. On August 4, 1914 Germany invaded Belgium, and officially kicked off what was to be forever labelled as World War I. The following spring, on May 7, 1915, another event took place which directly touched the troupe. It was the sinking of the passenger ship the Lusitania by German U-boats in the Atlantic Ocean. At the time, The Four Marx Brothers were in Toronto, Canada, in *Home Again*. Since they were of German descent, and suddenly Germans were seen as international villains, Groucho was forced to change his on-stage character from German-accented to Yiddish.

On September 2, 1915, a very unique thing happened in the career of The Marx Brothers. It was in Flint, Michigan, at the Majestic Theatre, that an audience was treated to the only known official performance of all five Marx Brothers! For a brief time, Minnie's premonition had come true.

According to the next day's issue of *The Flint Daily Journal*, 'The Four Marx Brothers, Julius, Milton, Leonard and Arthur, who have on many occasions delighted Flint patrons of vaudeville, opened another three days' engagement at the Majestic yesterday. For this occasion, however, there is a fifth Marx brother in the company. Master Herbert Marx, a lad of about 14, who gives promise of becoming as much of a favourite as the rest of the family. Master Herbert added some four or five songs to the rest of the program last night in a manner which left no doubt as to his future.' (20)

It was during this same era that The Marx Brothers first received the nicknames by which the world has come to know them. Apparently it came during a backstage poker game in Galesburg, Illinois. The person who named them "Groucho," "Chico," "Harpo" and "Gummo," was a man named Art Fisher, who was known as being a monologist or stand-up comedian. As he dealt them each their cards that day, he called them by the names which would forever stick to them.

Julius was named "Groucho" for his cynical manner, and for his tightly-held grouch bag. A grouch bag was a Vaudeville name for a purse or pocket on a string, which would be worn around one's neck at all times, to contain money and other valuables. Cash and jewellery and important personal items were not things that an actor would want to leave unattended in a dressing room or a changing area, while he or she was on stage.

Leo Marx was nicknamed "Chico" for his lust for women. According to legend, even when married, he would always be chasing after chicks. "Harpo" was to become Arthur/Adolph's stage name, due to his instrumental ability on the harp. The harp that he learned to play on was the one which was left to him when his maternal grandmother passed away.

Milton became known as "Gummo," because of the squeaky gum-soled shoes he favoured. On the wooden floors of theatrical stage, you could hear Gummo coming from far away because of the sound that his footwear would make when he walked.

It was some time later, after Herbert had joined his brothers in their act, that he received his name of "Zeppo." Minnie had purchased a farm for her family on which to live and work. According to one explanation, Herbert was sitting on a haystack one day, chewing on a piece of straw. As Chico walked by, Herbert said to him, "Howdy, Zeke." Chico looked back at him and said, "Howdy, Zep." After that the name Zeppo was to stick to him for all of his life. Groucho said later that airborne zeppelins were big the year that Herbert was born and Zeppo had come from his brother's interest in zeppelins.

From September 14, 1914 to August 1918, The Four Marx Brothers continued to tour around the country with their appealing hit show, *Home Again*. In late 1914, Minnie ran into a few problems with her management company. When The Marx Brothers missed a performance, her management company was sued and she lost the case. The court demanded that she pay $350 in damages. Instead of paying, she filed for bankruptcy.

Meanwhile, amidst the long run of their touring show, *Home Again*, America was finally drawn into World War I, when the country suddenly declared war on Germany on April 6, 1917.

There appears to be a bit of planned confusion as to why the four draft-age Marx boys were not drawn into military service. Both Groucho and Harpo, in their subsequent published biographies, breezed over the war. Groucho's book, *The Groucho Phile*, published in 1976 mentioned the sinking of the Lusitania, but jumped over the war years. It doesn't take a lot of delving into the facts to come up with the reasoning for Minnie Marx not wanting her boys to be drafted into the military service to fight in World War I. Since they had many friends and relatives still living in Germany, the idea of her boys killing their own countrymen was a horrifying prospect.

Seeking a solution to this problem, Minnie thought long and hard about the options. Finally, she came up with a foolproof scheme. She discovered that farmers, who had the responsibility of feeding the citizens of the United States, were completely exempt from military service. So, what did she do? You guessed it: she bought a farm!

Purchasing a farm in the Chicago area, in LaGrange, Illinois, seemed like a perfect ploy. As newly-christened gentlemen farmers, The Marx Brothers went from hatching routines on the vaudeville stage, to selling eggs from their chicken farm. Reportedly, the farm was one huge money-losing scheme from the very start. Apparently the rats ate all of the hen's eggs, so that when people came to purchase eggs from the Marx farm, the inexperienced farmers had to resort to some less than natural farming techniques. According to the book, *Monkey Business: The Lives And Legends Of The Marx Brothers*, egg buyers were startled to find that Rhode Island Red chickens - which normally lay brown eggs, would have white eggs underneath them. What had happened was that The Marx Brothers had to go to the store and purchased eggs to put under the chickens to keep their farming ruse intact.

In *The Groucho Phile*, which Groucho penned with Hector Arce, he explained that the brothers' routines were not at all typical for farmers. It was anything but the old adage of "early to bed and early to rise" on the Marx farm. 'The first morning on the farm,' recalled Groucho, 'we got up at five [o'clock a.m.]. The following morning we dawdled in bed until six. By the end of the week we were getting up at noon, which was just enough time for us to get dressed to catch the 1:07 to Wrigley Field where the Chicago Cubs played.' (3)

While Minnie bought the farm as a ploy to keep her sons away from the trenches of World War I, on October 31, 1918, exactly eleven days before peace was declared, Gummo Marx enlisted in the army! Gummo had long been discontented with his life on the stage. Now that The Marx Brothers' act was becoming less and less a song and dance act, and more and more a straight play with comic routines, Gummo was growing increasingly restless to get on with his own life. He saw enlisting in the army as the perfect way to leave the act behind him. With Gummo out of The Marx Brothers, Zeppo was suddenly in.

Although Minnie was still very much in the picture as the Marx's stage mother, and unofficial manager, she was forced to retire her assumed moniker of Minnie Palmer. It wasn't that this venture proved so depressingly unsuccessful in any way, it was that the real Minnie Palmer returned to the United States in 1918 to resume her own stage career. It is assumed that rather than risk being sued by the real Ms Palmer, Minnie Marx went back to being Minnie Marx.

And what of their father, Frenchy? Well, he was very much in the picture as well, as the boys' backstage caterer. Groucho was to recall of these days, 'When we were living in Chicago, and playing... the five [shows]-a-day houses, Frenchy would come into our dressing room after the final matinees, with a big basket of food... no restaurant could provide roast chicken or kugel like Frenchy's.' (21)

While in their routine of touring in *Home Again*, and being egg farmers by day, several other changes were occurring in The Marx Brothers' world. One of the biggest events of this era had been the first marriage of a Marx Brother. In March 1917, the troupe's prime womaniser, Chico, eloped and married Betty Karp. In January 1918, Chico and Betty celebrated the birth of their daughter, Maxine. From that point on, when The Marx Brothers toured, Maxine and Betty were part of the entourage as well.

When the war ended, Americans shifted their attention from the military conflict in Europe to amusing themselves in theatres and movie houses. In October 1918, The Four Marx Brothers debuted a new act, which they called *The Street Cinderella*. When it opened in October, it starred Groucho, Harpo, Chico and Gummo. However, come November 1, Gummo was replaced in the act by Zeppo.

Zeppo was later to confess, 'I never did care about show business. But my mother called me up to tell me that Gummo was leaving for the army and that she wanted to keep the name The Four Marx Brothers intact. She insisted I join the act, and that's what I did. I did not have a bit of experience in that I had done a little singing and dancing as a part of a cheap boy-and-girl act.' (2)

*The Street Cinderella* proved to be a big bust, and not nearly as crowd-pleasing as *Home Again* had been. In December 1918, The Four Marx Brothers revived *Home Again*, this time with Zeppo in the cast. As they struggled to find fresh material that suited their stage antics, at the first of the year they tried billing themselves as *The Marx Brothers Revue*, which they retooled and renamed *'N Everything*, which ran to the end of 1920.

On February 4, 1920, Groucho joined the ranks of the married Marxes, when he wed Ruth Johnson. Reportedly, Groucho was still so mad at his brother Chico for not inviting him to his elopement-style wedding in 1917, that he refused to invite him to his wedding to Ruth.

Later that same month, on February 13, while The Four Marx Brothers were on tour in Canada with *'N Everything*, their maternal grandfather, Levy Schönberg, died in New York City. Their tour with *'N Everything* continued until December 1920. During the run, the decision was made for the brothers to leave Chicago and move back to their home town: New York City.

# 5. The Road Back To Broadway

The brothers' next theatrical venture was a show they opened in February 1921 called *On The Mezzanine Floor*. It was to begin with a sequence in which each of the brothers would show up at the office of a theatrical manager, pitching ideas. This scene was later adapted and used as part of their hit Broadway show *I'll Say She Is*. It was captured on film, as a Paramount Pictures short promotional trailer called *The House That Shadows Built* (1931).

On July 21, 1921, Groucho and Ruth Marx celebrated the birth of their first child, Arthur. After years of being inseparable from each other, The Marx Brothers were finally having their own personal lives, complete with marriages and children.

Within months of debuting *On The Mezzanine Floor*, The Marx Brothers made some changes to it, and retitled the show *On The Balcony*. The show seemed to be a hit with audiences in New York City and throughout their tour across North America. They came to the conclusion that the time was right to take their brand of comedy to the other side of the Atlantic Ocean. On June 4, 1922, The Four Marx Brothers set sail on the SS Mauretania, headed for England.

Unfortunately, the audiences in London were less than impressed with The Four Marx Brothers or their play *On The Balcony*. The reviews and audience reactions were so poor that mid-run the brothers shifted shows from *On The Balcony* to *Home Again*. That didn't fare much better. In London, *The Times* pointed out disdainfully, that the humour of The Marx Brothers 'seems to be a little too trans-Atlantic for English audiences.' (22)

Back in the United States by the fall of 1922, The Four Marx Brothers decided that they needed to put a fire under their luke-warm careers, and produce their own silent film. It seemed to be all the rage, and who better to become stars of the silent screen than them?

According to Groucho, from the vantage point of 1933: 'Chico, Zeppo and I each contributed $1,000; and similar amounts came from the author, Jo Swerling, and two friends who would rather be nameless, although their names are Al Posen and Max Lippman. To be sure, the art and business of making movies were profound mysteries to all of us, especially Jo, who, maybe because of this, has since become a celebrated Hollywood author. But our lack of knowledge and experience did not keep us from getting ahead. And go ahead we did, to Fort Lee, New Jersey, where somehow or other the picture got itself finished.' (9)

The film was called *Humour Risk*, and a huge risk was what it was from the very beginning. Since the bulk of The Marx Brothers' best material is based in witty dialogue and double entendres, if is daunting to imagine how it would play on the silent screen, with only intermittent dialogue boxes to keep the story flowing. They enlisted several of their actor friends, including several of the cast members of their play *'N Everything*. Mildred Davis, the actress who later married silent-film comedian Harold Lloyd, appeared in *Humour Risk* as well. Groucho explained of the thin plot, 'I was the old movie villain, Harpo was the Love Interest - and these weren't the only things wrong with the production.' (9)

According to several sources, daily rushes of the filmed action were never viewed, they simply filmed a scene and moved on to the next one. No time or money was wasted on reshooting anything. The other huge obstacle was finding a distributor. Without a proper distributor, you may as well screen your film in your own basement. The Marx Brothers knew nothing about selling their film to a distributor. Finally, after wondering what to do about it, they found a theatre that would at least let them have a screening for industry insiders, to see if they could gain a distributor.

'So the seven cheerless producers gathered in the projection room with notebooks, cigars and heavy hearts,' Groucho remembered. 'None of us was very hopeful about the proceedings, but we said, without really believing our words, that, "You can't tell until an audience sees it. We'll get the thing previewed in some theatre around New York and then we'll know if we've got a picture or not." But we knew what we had, and so did the managers who viewed *Humour Risk*. Not one of them wanted the picture shown in his theatre. We even offered to pay a small rental, but the managers seemed to be too considerate of their audiences. It was Chico - it's always Chico - who found a weak-willed exhibitor in the Bronx who was willing to let us show our picture in the afternoon, when the audience consisted of backward children.' (9)

Needless to say, *Humour Risk* proved to be a financial risk for anyone involved in it. For the time being it was to languish gathering dust.

From September 1922 to March 1923, The Four Marx Brothers toured with the Shubert vaudeville unit, travelling from town to town as a featured act on the bill. Unable to properly take the reins of their career themselves, they decided that it was in their best interests to let the Shuberts deal with all of the details of bookings for them. The brothers then founded their own company, The Betty Amusement Company, to handle their business affairs. It was named after Chico's wife, Betty.

The material they performed on this vaudeville revue was - like a wedding - something old, something new, something borrowed and something blue. Harpo came up with a new routine in which he inflated a rubber glove and pretended to be milking a cow with the glove's swollen fingers. This was a routine which was later filmed for *A Night At The Opera*. An old routine, where a cop shakes down Harpo, only to unearth several place settings of silverware, was borrowed from *Home Again*. Once a routine worked for the four brothers, it was revived again and again. Many of the bits which looked hilariously fresh on film in the 1930s Marx Brothers films, were often several years old.

Unfortunately, while The Four Marx Brothers were on tour in the heartlands of the United States, the Shubert organisation was facing financial trouble and lawsuits. Caught in the crossfire, *The Twentieth Century Review*, complete with the four Marxes, went bankrupt in Indianapolis, Indiana, on March 7, 1923.

According to the March 8, 1923 issue of *Variety* newspaper, in an article entitled 'Unit Show with $60 In Box Office, Attached,' 'a deputy sheriff arrived and attached the box office, scenery and costumes of *The Twentieth Century Review*. The performance was called off and The Four Marx Brothers, owner of The Betty Amusement Company, are trying to work out the indebtedness.' (23)

Left high and dry in Indianapolis, The Four Marx Brothers were at a serious crossroads. What should they do? What were their options? Was it time to just pull the plug on the act and call it quits? Fortunately for all of us, the answer to this question was "no."

Apparently, the Shubert Organisation had The Marx Brothers under contract, and they weren't about to let them go. They also had a play that stalled in Philadelphia called *Love For Sale*, which was retooled and renamed *Give Me A Thrill*. It had stalled at the Walnut Theatre, with all of its sets and props and scenery intact, and no stars for it. Why not force the Marx boys into it, and let them add some mayhem and double talk to the script, and see if it flies? Well, in a nutshell, that's exactly what was done.

According to the May 3, 1923 issue of *Variety*, 'The Four Marx Brothers will head Philly's first summer revue, aimed for the Walnut Street Theatre, May 29. Will and Tom Johnstone are writing the show, which is produced by Joseph M Gaites and JM Beury. The attraction may be called *You Must Come Over*. Gaites favours four-word titles, they having been lucky for him with his *Take It From Me* and *Up In The Clouds*. Both the later shows were by the Johnstones.' (24)

Well it was a huge gamble. But somehow - against all odds - it paid off big time. Naturally, it went through quite a bit of retooling and rewriting once The Four Marx Brothers came into the picture. The name was also changed to take the four-word concurrently popular phrase of the day: *I'll Say She Is*. The plot of *I'll Say She Is* was completely scandalous adult-themed entertainment. It centres around a society woman who is in search of the perfect thrill. Man after man attempts to introduce her to the ultimately thrilling experience. When one gentleman takes her to an opium den for a kick, she becomes accidentally implicated in the stabbing death of someone, and finds herself up on trial for murder. Her legal counsel is none other than the smart-mouthed Groucho Marx. One bit of dialogue from *I'll Say She Is* was as follows:

Groucho: "You are going to be convicted of murder."

Beauty: "What makes you so confident?"

Groucho: "I'm going to be your lawyer!"

Once the Beauty was on the stand in court, she was questioned again by her lawyer: Groucho: "Why were you smoking opium in a Chinese joint?"

Beauty: "Because I wanted to get a new sensation."

Groucho: "Did you ever eat a bowl of rhubarb in a Ferris wheel?"

These snippets of dialogue give one an idea of the witty brand of insanity that must have ensued on stage during the run of this play.

When the local Philadelphia newspaper, *The Public Ledger*, reviewed the show in its June 5, 1923 issue, they headlined the article '*I'll Say She Is* Has Propitious Opening.' According to that review, 'The Four Marx Brothers are inimitable in all that they have to do. Occasionally one wishes that they were given more leeway, but when Arthur did remarkable things on the harp and [Leo] Marx performed on a piano with unbelievable dexterity, there was little to complain of; and Julius Marx, impersonating Napoleon, had moments of gutsy humour... *I'll Say She Is* has all the earmarks of a sturdy success, a success it will win by aid of jazz and plenty of dancing and pretty girls, and not by amazing novelty, really funny comedy or any degree of subtle imaginative material.' (25)

A smash in Philadelphia, it bombed in Boston and Washington DC, but it was a solid hit in Chicago, Kansas City, and Buffalo, New York. With a huge hit on their hands, finally - after all they had been through - they were ready for a bona fide Broadway hit. And, when the show opened at the Casino Theatre on the 'Great White Way,' that's exactly what they got! At long last - The Four Marx Brothers had finally arrived!

But, what would the potentially vicious New York City critics think of *I'll Say She Is*? Well, judging by Alexander Wollcott's review of the show in *The New York Sun*, they loved it. According to Wollcott's review, entitled 'Harpo Marx And Some Brothers: Hilarious Antics Spread Good Cheer At The Casino,' it had been worth the wait. Wrote Wollcott, 'As one of the many who laughed immodestly throughout the greater part of the first performance given by a new musical show, entitled, if memory serves, *I'll Say She Is*, it behoves your correspondent to report the most comical moments vouchsafed to the first nighters in a month of Mondays. It is a bright, coloured and vehement setting for the goings-on of those talented cut-ups, The Four Marx Brothers. In particular, it is a splendacious and reasonably tuneful excuse for going to see that silent brother, that shy, unexpected, magnificent comic among the Marxes, who is recorded somewhere on a birth certificate as Arthur, but who is known to the adoring two-a-day as Harpo Marx.' (26)

Because Alexander Wollcott was a charter member of the intellectuals who hung out at the nearby Algonquin Hotel's fabled 'Round Table,' he had a lot of clout in New York City. And, partially because - according to Groucho - Wollcott had a romantic crush on Harpo, Harpo became an official member of this elite group. Also part of the Round Table set at that time was the acid-tongued Dorothy Parker, Robert Benchley, Edna Ferber, Tallulah Bankhead, Helen Hayes and George Kaufman. After years of 'schlepping' their way from one vaudeville fleabag theatre to another, The Four Marx Brothers were now Broadway stars, and their lives were never to be quite the same.

It is interesting to note that although in their inner circle, The Four Marx Brothers were fondly known as "Groucho," "Harpo," "Chico" and "Zeppo," in their stage billing they were still officially Julius, Arthur (Adolph), Leo and Herbert.

Aside from having a hit on their hands with *I'll Say She Is*, it also turned them from being struggling actors to becoming wealthy stars. They all moved to better residences and Zeppo bought himself a 40-foot-long boat to cruise around Long Island Sound. They could not only afford all of the luxuries in life that they had only dreamed of before, they could also support their parents in a luxurious style as well. The boys purchased their parents a new house in Little Neck on Long Island. Minnie didn't ever have to pretend to be Minnie Palmer anymore. Now, she was proud to be exactly who she was: Minnie Marx - mother of the stars.

It was around this time that Alexander Wollcott requested a viewing of The Marx Brothers' first film, *Humour Risk*. One of the investors, Al Posen, produced a film can, which contained the only known print of *Humour Risk* that existed. Unfortunately, it was the original negative of the film. After Wollcott viewed the film - in its negative state - it was never returned and The Marx Brothers did not come by to pick it up either. To this day, there is no known copy of *Humour Risk* either as a print or as a negative. Perhaps one day it will turn up preserved in the cold basement of someone in Fort Lee, New Jersey, as so often rare and long believed lost films do resurface from time to time.

According to legend, Groucho Marx's famed painted-on moustache dates back to *I'll Say She Is*. He had been wearing artificial stage moustaches since his days of playing Mr Green in *Fun In Hi Skule* and *Mr Green's Reception*. One night he was so late at arriving at the theatre, the he simply stuck his finger in some black greasepaint, ran it across his upper lip and made his first entrance. The exaggerated black painted-on moustache was to become a lifelong trademark. With the moustache, the cigar and the ill-fitting top coat, Groucho's film persona was cemented in place.

# 6. The First Films

In 1925, Harpo Marx became the first brother to successfully break into the movies. He went out to Astoria Studios in Queens to visit friends of his who were working on a silent movie, and they asked him if he wanted to play a featured part. He gladly agreed. The film was *Too Many Kisses*, and it starred Richard Dix, Frances Howard and William Powell. Harpo played the role of the Village Peter Pan. The film didn't become a huge box-office smash but gave him a legitimate start as a movie actor.

The film, long considered missing, turned up several years ago, and footage from it can be seen in the documentary *The Unknown Marx Brothers* on DVD. Harpo, dressed in a tunic and cross-laced boots, is seen confronting one of the film's villains and speaking his only lines of dialogue on film. However, this was a silent movie. Because of the existence of *Too Many Kisses*, it is possible to look back at Harpo's screen career and say that he is the only movie star who started in silent films, and became a star by remaining silent in talkies!

Life began to move at a much faster pace from this point on for The Four Marx Brothers. *I'll Say She Is* ran until 1925. By the end of that year, the boys continued to hold court on Broadway in their new show *The Cocoanuts*, which was specially written for them by George S Kaufman and his assistant, Morrie (Morris) Ryskind. In addition to The Four Marx Brothers, Kaufman and Ryskind had a new character to write into the plot. This character was someone the brothers could play off as a straight person to their lunatic jokes and stunts. She was a woman by the name of Margaret Dumont, and she was to effectively become the unofficial fifth Marx Brother.

Apparently, Margaret Dumont had already been through several career incarnations before she became a staple of The Marx Brothers' films. Of the 13 full-length feature films that The Marx Brothers starred in, Margaret Dumont was in seven. She was born Daisy Juliette Baker, in Brooklyn, New York, in 1882. In her younger days, she was a singer and showgirl. In 1920 she began doing character roles in Broadway shows, turning up in that year's musical comedy hit *Fifty Fifty* as well as George M Cohen's *Mary* (1920), *The Fan* (1921) and *Go Easy Mabel* (1921). She excelled at playing aristocratic ladies, which was what she primarily played in The Marx Brothers' comedies.

Reportedly, when *The Cocoanuts* ran during its out-of-town try-out in Philadelphia, it received a mixed reception. Each brother was worried that they were not getting enough laughs in the show, so they began ad libbing comic lines or physical comedy staging. Both George Kaufman and Morrie Ryskind were constantly startled by what they saw or heard on stage during the run of *The Cocoanuts*. Supposedly Kaufman turned to Ryskind during one such performance and commented, "Hush! I think I just heard a line from the script!" (27)

Following its Philadelphia and Boston runs, *The Cocoanuts* opened on Broadway, at the Lyric Theatre on December 9, 1925. It was another hit for the Marx boys, and it ran an impressive 377 performances.

This was the golden era of The Marx Brothers as Broadway stars. Chico's daughter, Maxine, would later write of watching her father and her famous uncles from the backstage. Speaking first of Uncle Harpo, Maxine recalled, 'I would watch him during intermission, his flaming red wig on a stand, furiously plucking on a harp he always kept in the corner of his dressing room so his fingers would stay tough (they would bleed if he didn't practice every day). He would have a big Turkish towel wrapped round his head because he perspired a lot under the wig, and was

44

worried that he would get a chill. Daddy most likely would be doing a crossword puzzle, muttering obscure words to himself. Groucho would be seated in the adjoining dressing room with his copy of *The Nation*, composing obscene letters to the editor, while Zeppo would be on the phone trying to get a date.' (28)

Groucho and Ruth and little Arthur were able to move out of their apartment on the Upper West Side of Manhattan to a lovely house in Great Neck, Long Island. On May 19, 1927, Groucho and Ruth Marx's second child, Miriam, was born.

After its Broadway run, The Marx Brothers took *The Cocoanuts* out on the road, and toured across the United States. Now that they were making more money, it spelled security for Groucho and Harpo and Zeppo. For Chico however, it simply meant that he had more money to gamble with, and get deeper in debt. While they were in Detroit with *The Cocoanuts*, Chico took off one night and went into hiding for a couple of days. Apparently he had lost a great deal of money in New York City and owed a gambling debt to some gangsters who were trailing him. When he finally returned, his brothers were furious with him. According to Maxine, Groucho told Chico's wife, Betty, "I'm not going to forgive him for this one... He should have said something to me. I knew the bastard needed some dough. Instead of trusting me, he makes everybody think he's wearing a block of cement at the bottom of a lake. I don't know how you can stand him, Betty, I really don't." (28) This was not the first of Chico's gambling troubles, and it was not his last.

The Four Marx Brothers were on a roll now. On October 23, 1928, *Animal Crackers*, The Marx Brothers third successive hit musical, opened on Broadway. The show was again written by George S Kaufman and Morrie Ryskind. One of the truly inspired creations from *Animal Crackers* is Groucho's outlandish character of Captain Spaulding ("One morning I shot an elephant in my pyjamas. How he got into my pyjamas, I'll never know,") the African explorer.

It was at this point when the movies finally caught up with The Marx Brothers. Motion pictures with sound had suddenly become all the rage. When the 1927 Al Jolson feature *The Jazz Singer* debuted with actual dialogue and songs in it, silent pictures were clearly destined to become obsolete. Movie companies were suddenly scrambling to get in on this latest craze. Not only did they need actors who could speak dialogue believably, but they also needed scripts.

Paramount Pictures signed The Four Marx Brothers to a five-picture deal. Paramount were in such a hurry to produce the first film that the boys filmed *The Cocoanuts* on Long Island during the day while performing in *Animal Crackers* on Broadway at night.

## *The Cocoanuts (1929)*

*The Crew:* Robert Florey (Director/Choreography), Joseph Santley (Director/Choreography), Monta Bell (Producer), James R Cowan (Producer), Walter Wanger (Producer), George Kaufman (Screenwriter/ Composer Music Score), Morris Ryskind (Screenwriter/Composer Music Score), George Folsey (Cinematographer), Irving Berlin (Composer Music Score), Barney Rogan (Editor), Frank Tours (Musical Direction/ Supervision).

*The Cast:* Groucho Marx (Mr Hammer), Harpo Marx (Harpo), Chico Marx (Chico), Zeppo Marx (Jamison), Mary Eaton (Polly Potter), Oscar Shaw (Bob Adams), Margaret Dumont (Mrs Potter), Cyril Ring (Harvey Yates), Kay Francis (Penelope Martin), Barton MacLane (Bather), Basil Ruysdael (Hennessy). 96 minutes

*The Story:* Mr Hammer is the manager of a hotel in Florida where things are so bad that he cannot even pay the staff. The only guest in the whole hotel who is actually paying her bill is Mrs Potter. Her daughter Polly loves up-and-coming new architect Bob. Mrs Potter prefers that Polly marry Harvey Yates instead. Unbeknown to Mrs Potter is the fact that he is actually a jewel thief sizing her up. Harvey's accomplice in crime is slinky Penelope. Amidst this plot, Groucho, Harpo, Chico and Zeppo bumble their way through one mishap after another.

*Funniest Scenes:* Groucho and Chico in their famous "viaduct" routine, where Chico keeps asking "Why a duck?" Harpo's classic sight gags include him eating the telephone on the hotel's front desk and washing it down with the ink from the inkwell. The "Monkey Doodle Do" song and dance number is amusing in its sheer silliness. Trying to sell lots of land at his Cocoanut paradise, Groucho claims of the housing plans: "You can get stucco. And HOW you can get stuck-o!"

*Behind The Scenes:* The filmed version of *The Cocoanuts* is considered a classic piece of cinema for many reasons. Not only is it the first full-length Marx Brothers' feature, but it is also a living record of what the brothers' original show on Broadway must have looked like. Basically, the set of the original Broadway show was reassembled at Astoria Studios in Queens, Long Island, and filmed in continuous takes. A lot of the filming suffers from stagebound shooting techniques, but it remains a time capsule of pure Marxian insanity. The musical numbers, which are intact in the film, should have been somehow restaged to depict the dancers' legs and feet more clearly. However, in an effort to capture entire scenes, long shots were used since extensive sound and motion editing was still technologically years away. If you look closely, you can see that the newspapers and maps are completely wet. This was done so that the sound of crinkling paper was not picked up by the microphones.

The whole filmed experience proved challenging for directors Robert Florey and Joseph Santley. According to Florey, "I had five cameras going at all times. One for a long master shot, one for a medium shot and three for close-ups. If one or even two of the brothers went out of range, I could always cut to a close-up to compensate for the missing member." (2)

*Little-Known Fact:* This is the only Marx Brothers' comedy where Harpo appears to be wearing a dark wig on camera. He was wearing the shocking red one that he wore on stage. After this film, he changed to a blonde wig, because the red one photographed so much darker.

*Verdict:* Although *The Cocoanuts* is stagy in look and sound, it is a brilliant look at the kind of theatrical lunacy that made them such a hit on Broadway. There is an exuberance and an innocence to The Marx Brothers which makes this a must-see romp for any Marx fan. 3/5

On May 3, 1929, the filmed version of *The Cocoanuts* had its premiere in New York City at the Rialto Theatre. Minnie had finally seen her boys become movie stars. Then on September 13, 1929, the indomitable Minnie Marx suffered a seizure and she passed away at two o'clock on the morning of September 14 at the age of 65.

Still not over the loss of their dear mother, The Marx Brothers were hit with another catastrophe - along with the rest of the United States - when the stock market crashed on what is now known as Black Friday, in October 1929. Both Groucho and Harpo had invested heavily in the stock market, and they suffered great financial losses.

The Marx Brothers' transfer from Broadway to film was well timed. Box-office sales of Broadway shows suddenly took a huge loss. Whereas *The Cocoanuts* had headlined on Broadway for 377 performances, *Animal Crackers* was played out after only 171 performances. As they had done previously with *The Cocoanuts*, The Marx Brothers returned to Astoria Studios to film their second movie, *Animal Crackers*. It opened on August

25, 1930. Viewing these two films back to back, reveals their second cinematic adventure to be a much more assured affair.

## *Animal Crackers (1930)*

*The Crew:* Victor Heerman (Director), Bert Kalmar (Screenwriter/Composer Music Score), Harry Ruby (Screenwriter/Composer Music Score/Songwriter), Morris Ryskind (Screenwriter), George Folsey (Cinematographer).

*The Cast:* Groucho Marx (Capt. Jeffrey T Spaulding), Harpo Marx (The Professor), Chico Marx (Signor Emmanuel Ravelli), Zeppo Marx (Horatio Jamison), Lillian Roth (Arabella Rittenhouse), Margaret Dumont (Mrs Rittenhouse), Louis Sorin (Roscoe W Chandler), Hal Thompson (John Parker), Margaret Irving (Mrs Whitehead), Kathryn Reece (Grace Carpenter), Richard Greig (Hives), Edward Metcalf (Inspector Hennessey), The Music Masters (Six Footmen). 98 minutes

*The Story:* On her Long Island Estate, wealthy Mrs Rittenhouse throws a weekend party where she plans to unveil an expensive painted masterpiece. To liven up the proceedings she invites the famous African explorer, Jeffrey T Spaulding to entertain and delight her guests. Also present for the nonsense are noted musician Signor Emmanuel Ravelli, the girl-chasing "Professor", and Spaulding's faithful - but confused - secretary Horatio Jamison. While the guests are present, Mrs Rittenhouse's daughter Arabella decides to play a trick on her, by replacing the painting with a fake.

*Funniest Scenes:* The nonsensical monologue in which Groucho Marx talks about his adventures in deepest, darkest Africa is priceless, and obviously reveals that the closest he has ever come to Africa is perhaps an afternoon at the Bronx Zoo. Harpo and Chico are a riot cheating at bridge. Groucho dictating an insane letter to befuddled Zeppo, addressed to Hungerdunger, Hungerdunger, Hungerdunger and McCormick.

*Verdict:* Although *Animal Crackers* is as stagy as *The Cocoanuts* was before it, in the year between the two films, the sound equipment, technology and camerawork were all far superior. *Animal Crackers* is pure lunacy. 4/5

In February 1931, lured out to the West Coast by their new-found success in the film business, The Marx Brothers officially moved to Hollywood. Broadway had given them three solid stage hits in a row, and it was now time to devote their energies to living the lives of movie stars.

From the very beginning, The Marx Brothers' act was aimed at adults. Many of the plot lines and themes of their humour contained either sexual references or were double entendres. Their witty dialogue usually went over the heads of children. When their movies were suddenly transferred to film, Hollywood imposed several restrictions upon their scripts and filmed content.

It is interesting to note that even back in the early 1930s a vast majority of the films in release were gangster movies with lots of shooting and killing. Groucho was later to recall, 'I remember, too, the day when my son Arthur - he was seven years old at that time - walked out on our first successful movie, *The Cocoanuts*, because the picture contained no shooting. It depressed me - not so much because he didn't care for the movie, but I was afraid he was going to become a critic when he grew up.' (9)

As Janice Anderson pointed out in her 1985 book, *The History Of Movie Comedy*, *The Cocoanuts* (1929) and *Animal Crackers* (1930)... These early movies were terribly stagebound, cluttered up with 'romantic' male singers and musical 'interludes,' and directed in a very ham-fisted style, but even so, The Marx Brothers' talent showed through it all, and more than one film critic saw that here were clowns of great potential.' (29)

# 7. Hooray For Hollywood

Newly ensconced in Hollywood, The Marx Brothers began work on their first all-new movie, *Monkey Business*.

## *Monkey Business (1931)*

*The Crew:* Norman Z McLeod (Director), Herman Mankiewicz (Producer), Arthur Sheekman (Screenwriter), SJ Perelman (Screenwriter), Arthur Todd (Cinematographer).

*The Cast:* Groucho Marx (Stowaway), Chico Marx (Chico), Harpo Marx (Harpo), Zeppo Marx (Zeppo), Thelma Todd (Lucille), Tom Kennedy (First Officer Gibson), Ruth Hall (Mary Helton), Rockliffe Fellowes (Joe Helton), Harry Woods (Alky Briggs), Maxine Castle (Opera Singer Madame Swempski), Otto H Fries (Second Mate), Evelyn Pierce (Manicurist), Ben Taggart (Captain Corcoran). 77 minutes

*The Story:* The Marx Brothers play four stowaways on a luxury ocean liner, bound for New York. While the boys try to escape from the ship's crew, and the especially dim First Mate Gibson, each of the brothers has a series of misadventures on ship. Groucho somehow gets himself in the middle of the affair between gangster Alky Briggs and Briggs' "babe" of a wife Lucille. Retired bootlegger Joe Helton hires Chico as his personal bodyguard, while Zeppo romances Joe's daughter Mary. Once they've smuggled themselves on shore in New York, The Marx Brothers make their way to Helton's Long Island mansion, where the insanity continues.

*Funniest Scenes:* The Brothers Marx as stowaways in barrels is classic. Harpo trying to hide inside a Punch & Judy puppet show, where he impersonates one of the puppets, is very funny. In a sequence borrowed from their own *I'll Say She Is*, each of the Marx boys tries to debark and get through customs by impersonating Maurice Chevalier, whose passport they have swiped.

*Behind The Scenes:* Although it uses many of the quartets most famous bits from the stage, this is the first Marx Brothers movie penned directly for the screen. Look for the boys' father in the scene where the ship docks - he is not only arriving on the ship, but in the next shot he can be spotted meeting himself on shore!

*Verdict:* By now, The Marx Brothers truly have the experience and know-how to play effectively to a cinema camera instead of a live stage audience. They were really hitting their stride on this film, which is one of their finest. It was released on September 19, 1931, to great success. 4/5

## *Horse Feathers (1932)*

*The Crew:* Norman Z McLeod (Director), Herman Mankiewicz (Producer), Bert Kalmar (Screenwriter), SJ Perelman (Screenwriter), Harry Ruby (Screenwriter/Composer Music Score), Ray June (Cinematographer).

*The Cast:* Groucho Marx (Professor Quincy Adams Wagstaff), Chico Marx (Baravelli), Harpo Marx (Pinky), Zeppo Marx (Frank Wagstaff), Thelma Todd (Connie Bailey aka The College Widow), David Landau (Jennings), Florine McKinney (Peggy Carrington), James Pierce (Mullen), Reginald Barlow (Retiring President of Huxley College), EH Calvert (Professor in Wagstaff's Study), Robert Greig (The Biology Professor), Edward J Le Saint (Professor), Nat Pendleton (MacHardie). 67 minutes

*The Story:* Professor Quincy Adams Wagstaff is being sworn in as the new president of Huxley College. While delivering his acceptance speech, he launches in to a song and dance number, proclaiming that whatever it is that is suggested to him, 'I'm Against It.' One of the students at the college is his son, Frank, who has been enrolled at the school for 12 years. Frank tells him that there has been a new president of the school every year since 1888, and that the only way to save the school is to win the upcoming football season. To assure a win, he goes to the local speakeasy where two of the better football heroes hang out.

Unfortunately, he hires the wrong men: Baravelli, the ice man/ bootlegger, and Pinky the local dog catcher. Local gambler Jennings has all his bets on Darwin College in the forthcoming Thanksgiving Day football game. He gets his girlfriend, Connie - who is known as the "college widow" to steal the secret signals from the opposing team. Each of the four Marx Brothers arrives at Connie's apartment to court her. In separate scenes, each of The Marx Brothers serenade her with the song 'Everyone Says I Love You.' The big football game finale is the height of Marx Brothers craziness.

*Funniest Scenes:* The speakeasy scene, where Groucho tries to pry the entry password out of Chico, is priceless. The password was "swordfish," and it is side-splittingly funny when Harpo shows up to give the password in pantomime - with a sword and a real fish. While giving a lecture, Groucho points to a picture of a horse's ass and announces, "That reminds me, I haven't seen my son all day." When Thelma Todd falls out of a canoe being paddled by Groucho she calls for a "life saver." He extracts a roll of Lifesaver candies from his pocket and tosses her one. This is the best Zeppo Marx performance on film, finding him at his matinee idol best.

*Behind The Scenes:* As witnessed in *Horse Feathers*, Harpo Marx was truly a link between the great silent-film actors of the past and the modern "talkies" of the 1930s.

Other than Margaret Dumont, the one woman who appeared in more than one Marx Brothers film was beautiful actress Thelma Todd (real life nickname: Hot Toddy). She appeared in *Monkey Business* and *Horse Feathers*. Ironically, her role as gangster wife Lucille Briggs in *Monkey Business* echoed Todd's real life – she was known to associate with gangsters. Eventually, she owned and ran her own restaurant in Santa Monica. Under shady circumstances, on December 16, 1935, Thelma Todd was found dead in her car, in her own garage. Her death was ruled to be due to carbon monoxide inhalation. It was never proven, but it has long been believed that she had got herself too deeply involved with the secret doings of her gangster boyfriends, and was murdered. At one point in *Monkey Business*, Groucho says to Todd, "You're a woman who's been getting nothing but dirty breaks. Well, we can clean and tighten your brakes, but you'll have to stay in the garage all night."

*Verdict:* One of the funniest of all of The Marx Brothers' movies. The situations, the performances and the one-liners propel this one over the goalpost with humour and panache. Released on August 10, 1932, *Horse Feathers* was such a hit that the boys ended up on the cover of *Time* magazine - in the garbage cart/chariot from the riotous football game finale of the film. 5/5

Not everything went smoothly for The Marx Brothers in Hollywood. While filming *Horse Feathers*, Chico was in a car crash in which he hurt his knee and fractured a couple of his ribs. Consequently, the filming of the big football game climax had to be postponed while he recuperated. Zeppo, now married to Marion, divided his time between a Malibu beach house and an apartment on Havenhurst Drive in Hollywood. In August 1932 their Havenhurst apartment was robbed of $37,500 in jewellery and possessions. On May 11, 1933, The Marx Brothers' dear father, Samuel "Frenchy" Marx, died. The following month, Zeppo and Marion were again robbed, this time at gunpoint.

It was not all bad news as The Marx Brothers began to adjust to their new West Coast lifestyle. In November 28, 1932, Groucho and Chico, longing for some outlet other than movies to spread their unique brand of humour, began appearing on a regular NBC radio series. It was called *Flywheel, Shyster And Fly-*

*wheel*, and it gave them the opportunity to try out new comedy bits in front of a studio audience.

On November 22, 1933, the fifth, and most memorable Marx Brothers' film, *Duck Soup*, was released. Although it is now revered as a classic film, at the time of its release the film did not do as well at the box office as their previous four.

## *Duck Soup (1933)*

*The Crew:* Leo McCarey (Director), Herman Mankiewicz (Producer), Bert Kalmar (Screenwriter), Nat Perrin (Screenwriter), Harry Ruby (Screenwriter/Songwriter), Arthur Sheekman (Screenwriter), Henry Sharp (Cinematographer), LeRoy Stone (Editor), Hans Dreier (Art Director), Wiard Ihnen (Art Director), Arthur Johnston (Musical Direction/ Supervision).

*The Cast:* Groucho Marx (Rufus T Firefly), Chico Marx (Chicolini), Harpo Marx (Pinky), Zeppo Marx (Bob Rolland), Margaret Dumont (Mrs Teasdale), Raquel Torres (Vera Marcal), Louis Calhern (Ambassador Trentino), Verna Hillie (Trentino's Secretary), Leonid Kinskey (Agitator), Edmund Breese (Zander), Edwin Maxwell (Secretary Of War), Edgar Kennedy (Lemonade Seller), William Worthington (First Minister of Finance), Davison Clark (Second Minister of Finance), George MacQuarrie (First Judge), Eric Mayne (Third Judge), Fred Sullivan (Second Judge), Charles B Middleton (Prosecutor). 70 minutes

*The Story:* The mythical tiny country of Freedonia is in financial trouble again. Wealthy Mrs Teasdale is called upon to bail out the treasury to the tune of $20 million. She reluctantly agrees, but only if she chooses the new leader of the country. The country's ministers agree and she appoints - of all people - Rufus T Firefly. When Firefly shows up for his own swearing in, he is late, surly, insulting and obviously inept. The leader of neighbouring country, Sylvania, Ambassador Trentino, sees this as the opportunity to take over Freedonia. He hatches a scheme to discredit Firefly and sends two spies to gather evidence: Pinky and Chicolini. No one can talk any sense into Firefly, least of all his secretary Bob Rolland. In a completely insane move, Firefly declares war on Sylvania.

*Funniest Scenes:* Harpo has a riotous war of wits with a man running a lemonade stand, played by comedy actor Edgar Kennedy. Groucho is at his pompous best, donning an American Confederate General's outfit in one of the war scenes. At one point, Chico defects to the Freedonia side because the food is better. And, Harpo wears a sandwich board onto the battlefield which reads: 'Join the Army and See the Navy.' Making a mockery of all wars, The Four Marx Brothers even lampoon the American Revolutionary war in a fantasy sequence.

*Behind The Scenes:* The whole movie points out the hypocrisy of war, whilst war was brewing in real-life Europe.

*Verdict:* Brilliant! A must-see Marx classic comedy from start to finish. 5/5


The Four Marx Brothers were now so popular that they were immortalised in Hollywood film lore when they were asked to leave their footprints in cement in front of Graumann's Chinese Theatre on Hollywood Boulevard. However, based on the poor performance of *Duck Soup* at the box office, Paramount did not renew The Marx Brothers' contract.

While all of this was happening, Harpo had projects of his own underway. In 1933 he became the first American performer since the First World War to make a personal appearance tour of Russia. What few people realise is that Harpo carried top secret documents back from Europe which he passed on to the American government. While passing through Nazi-controlled Germany, he saw first-hand the anti-Semitism that was sweeping through the country. Harpo ventured into one establishment in Hamburg, which had the word 'Jude' (Jew) written on the wall in graffiti. According to him, 'Inside, behind half-empty counters, people in a daze, cringing like they didn't know what hit them and didn't know where the next blow would come from. Hitler had been in power only six months, and his boycott was already in full effect. I hadn't been so wholly conscious of being a Jew since my bar mitzvah. It was the first time since I'd had the measles that I was too sick to eat.' (10)

The following year was to be a transitional time for The Marx Brothers. On March 4, 1934, Groucho and Chico Marx began a new radio program, *The Marx Of Time*, for CBS Radio. On March 30, 1934, Zeppo Marx officially quit as one of The Marx Brothers. He had been unhappy with his role in the act, and for a long time he felt that he was the weakest link in the comedy team.

While they sorted things out with their business affairs, Groucho briefly returned to the legitimate stage. This time around it was far from the lights of Broadway, it was an appearance in the play *Twentieth Century* in summer stock in Maine. He played the role of Jaffe, the Broadway producer.

Back in Hollywood, it was Chico who came up with their new movie deal. It just so happened that Irving Thalberg, the head of production at MGM Studios, was a bridge-playing partner of Chico's. Over cards one night, Chico told Irving that he didn't think that The Marx Brothers' career was over yet. Thalberg agreed, decided to sign the act to MGM and to oversee their career personally.

However, when Chico presented the MGM deal to his brothers Harpo and Groucho, they refused to sign the contracts. When Chico asked what the problem was, they informed him that they refused to sign the contracts, unless he turned over his finances to them to manage for him. They were tired of watching Chico waste all of his hard-earned money on gambling. He had no choice but to agree. With that, all three signed to MGM, for what was to turn out to be their second great era of film-making. The first two films that Irving Thalberg helmed for his studio were two of the most memorable: *A Night At The Opera* and *A Day At The Races*.

At first, Groucho was reportedly a bit put off by Thalberg's haughtiness towards them. He told the brothers Marx that he thought their last film, *Duck Soup*, was a turkey. According to Groucho, 'I was a little annoyed by this, as I thought *Duck Soup* was a very funny picture and I told him so. "Yes," he said, "that's true, but the audience doesn't give a damn about you fellas. I can make a picture with you that would have half as many laughs as your Paramount films, but they will be more effective because the audience will be more in sympathy with you."' (2)

Irving Thalberg was married to Academy Award-winning actress Norma Shearer. Her brother, Douglas Shearer, excelled at - and was fascinated with - sound equipment. Douglas was directly responsible for the superior sound that MGM films possessed and, because The Marx Brothers were now at MGM, and their films were supervised by Thalberg, with sound by Douglas Shearer, their next two movies carried with them a marked improvement in their sound quality.

The Marx Brothers were convinced that they did their best work on camera when they were filming routines that they had tested on stage. MGM agreed to send them on a tour of movie theatres, to perform their new comedy routines in front of live audiences. It was a huge success, and when they returned to Hollywood they incorporated the new material into *A Night At The Opera*.

## *A Night At The Opera (1935)*

*The Crew:* Sam Wood (Director), Irving Thalberg (Producer), Al Boasberg (Screenwriter), Bert Kalmar (Screenwriter), George Kaufman (Screenwriter), Harry Ruby (Screenwriter), Morris Ryskind (Screenwriter), Merritt B Gerstad (Cinematographer), Herbert Stothart (Composer Music Score), William Le Vanway (Editor), Ben Carre (Art Director), Cedric Gibbons (Art Director), Edwin B Willis (Set Designer), Dolly Tree (Costume Designer), Chester Hale (Choreography), Douglas Shearer (Sound).

*The Cast:* Groucho Marx (Otis B Driftwood), Harpo Marx (Tomasso), Chico Marx (Fiorello), Margaret Dumont (Mrs Claypool), Kitty Carlisle (Rosa Castaldi), Walter Woolf King (Rodolpho Lassparri), Edward Keane (The Captain), Sig Rumann (Herman Gottlieb), Allan Jones (Ricardo Baroni), Robert E O'Connor (Detective Henderson), Harry Allen (Doorman), Al Bridge (Immigration Inspector), Gino Corrado (Steward), Otto H Fries (Elevator Man), Billy Gilbert (Engineer's Assistant), William Gould (Captain of Police), George Guhl (Policeman), Jonathan Hale (Stage Manager), Rodolfo Hoyos, Jr. (Count di Luna), George Irving (Committee), Selmar Jackson (Committee), Jack Lipson (Engineer's Assistant), Inez Palange (Maid), Claude Payton (Police Captain), Rolfe Sedan (Aviator), Leo White (Aviator), Jay Eaton (Aviator), Harry Tyler (Sign Painter), Frank Yaconelli (Engineer), Enrico Ricardi (Harpo's whistling double). 92 minutes

*The Story:* The film opens with Mrs Claypool in a restaurant, in the process of being stood up by her dinner partner. It turns out to be Otis B Driftwood, a promoter she has hired to introduce her into society. It is his plan to make her a patron of the opera. Driftwood introduces her to a snobbish opera entrepreneur named Gottlieb. Driftwood is also involved in the backstage doings of the local opera. He meets up with a man named Fiorello who is promoting a man he claims is the "world's greatest tenor." Driftwood thinks he is getting Rodolpho Lassparri but he is actually getting Fiorello's pal Ricardo Baroni. Groucho and Chico try to hammer out the contract, with comic results. The whole troupe then boards a ship bound from Europe to New York City, to present an opera. Once in New York, they wreak havoc on the opera house. Amidst all this, the two tenors battle for the affections of Rosa. Naturally, in the eleventh hour, Rosa and Ricardo end up the stars of the opera, once Groucho and Chico eliminate the dastardly Lassparri from the programme.

*Funniest Scenes:* Groucho and Chico going over the contract for a tenor ("The party of the first part shall hereafter be known as the party of the first part...") is a riot, and surely the inspiration for Abbot & Costello's "Who's on first?" routine. Harpo serving his brothers pancakes - then applying catsup as lipstick and powdered sugar as face powder with a pancake powder puff. Also, Harpo kissing everyone 'bon voyage' as the ship leaves. However, the funniest scene of all is Groucho's jam-packed miniature stateroom on the cruise ship - stuffed tighter than a sardine can with people.

*Verdict: A Night At The Opera* is one of the very best of The Marx Brothers' films, and was a high point of their film career. 5/5

*A Night At The Opera* was released on November 1, 1935, and it became a huge smash at the box office. Suddenly, The Marx Brothers were huge stars all over again, although this time they were without Zeppo. Although Zeppo was not in any of the remaining Marx Brothers' films, his position as straight man and romantic lead was played by a variety of young actors.

When it came time to begin work on their next film, *A Day At The Races*, The Marx Brothers again hit the road to do a performance tour to work out gags and dialogue. They toured all over the country, to Minneapolis, Chicago and San Francisco. After 141 stage performances, the boys finally felt that they were ready to go before the cameras. Filming began on September 3, 1936. Five days later, Irving Thalberg came down with a bad cold. His health deteriorated rapidly and then he died of pneumonia on September 14 at the age of 37. Production on *A Day At The Races* was shut down until December.

In the interim, Harpo got married to Susan Fleming. Without alerting the press, or his brothers, they got into the car, drove down to Santa Ana and were wed by a Justice Of The Peace in Santa Ana. Reportedly, the Justice Of The Peace office was located next to a firehouse, so the witnesses to the September 28 wedding were a fireman and his wife.

The seventh Marx Brothers' film went through a long series of rewrites during its production. Not only did the sudden death of Thalberg throw things into a spin, there were several versions of some scenes which finally appeared on the screen. Four screenplay writers worked on the film: Robert Pirosh, George Seaton, George Oppenheimer and an uncredited Al Boasberg. Reportedly, even George S Kaufman was involved in some of the scenes. One such scene was known in Seaton's notes as the 'Touting scene at track.' It is in this sequence, that one of the most famous Marx Brothers' scenes took place between Chico and Groucho. Relying heavily on his Italian accent, Chico attempts to sell Groucho "Tutsi-Frutsi ice cream" and a list of racing tips, which is so detailed that Groucho's horse has come in, in first place, and paid off before he is even given a chance to place his bet. Harpo was given his own elaborate musical number in the picture, appearing figuratively as Gabriel, and serenading the Black citizens of the imaginary town of Sparkling Springs Lake with his musicality. After all of this hard work, on June 11, 1937, *A Day At The Races* was finally released.

## *A Day At The Races (1937)*

*The Crew:* Irving Thalberg (Producer - uncredited), Sam Wood (Producer), Lawrence Weingarten (Producer), Sam Spiegel (Associate Producer), Sam Wood (Director), Robert Pirosh (Screenplay), George Seaton (Screenplay), George Oppenheimer (Screenplay), Al Boasberg (Screenplay - uncredited), Bronislau Kaper (Music Composer), Walter Jurmann (Music Composer), Gus Kahn (Lyrics), Franz Waxman (Musical Director), Dave Gould (Choreographer), Joseph Ruttenberg (Photography), Cedric Gibbons (Art Director), Stan Rogers (Art Director), Edwin B Willis (Sets), Douglas Shearer (Sound), Dolly Tree (Wardrobe), Frank E Hull (Film Editor).

*The Cast:* Groucho Marx (Dr Hugo Z Hackenbush), Harpo Marx (Stuffy), Chico Marx (Tony), Margaret Dumont (Mrs Upjohn), Siegfried Rumann (Dr Steinberg), Allan Jones (Gil), Maureen O'Sullivan (Judy Standish), Douglas Dumbrille (Morgan), Leonard Ceeley (Whitmore), Esther Muir (Flo Marlowe), Roberd Middlemass (Sheriff), Frankie Durro (Jockey), Pat Flaherty (Detective), Ivie Anderson & The Drinoline Choir (Singers), The Three Chocolateers, Plantation Boys, Four Hot Shots, Ben Carter, Darby Jones, Dorothy Dandridge, Gus Robinson and Buck Woods (Singers in Harpo's musical number). 111 minutes

*The Story:* Judy Standish is running a sanatorium in Sparkling Springs, where she is assisted by Tony. Judy is about to lose her prime client, wealthy hypochondriac Emily Upjohn. Emily wants to check out of the sanatorium because she wants to be treated by a certain Dr Hackenbush, who is an expert in her latest ailment. Tony enlists the support of Dr Hackenbush, but he gets the wrong one - Hugo Z Hackenbush, who is a veterinarian. Nearby is a racetrack, where one of the local jockeys is Stuffy. Stuffy refuses to throw a race when he is instructed to do so, which causes comic complications. When Tony brings Dr Hackenbush a new patient, Stuffy, the three brothers have a scene together that erupts into sheer silliness.

Although Judy knows that Hackenbush is a phoney, she keeps her mouth shut to keep Emily Upjohn as a paying client, and hence keep the sanatorium. When Tony and Stuffy are being chased by the crooked racetrack owner, they push their way into the Winter Carnival's orchestra, which becomes the perfect moment for Chico to play one of his entertaining piano solos. This one is of special note, as Harpo is seen - and heard - playing a piano duet with him. However, by the end of the number, he has broken away the body of the piano, and he ends playing the piano strings by hand - as though it was a harp. Harpo has a flute number in which he serenades a group of Black children, which turns into a great gospel number with the children's parents. It evolves further when Harpo stumbles into a Black jazz joint. Harpo and his flute make this one of the best and most creative musical numbers in all of their movies. Watch closely for Dorothy Dandridge in the musical scene too. Before the number is over, all three Marx Brothers join in, to do the jitterbug at the jazz festival. Naturally, the picture leads into an insane racecourse scene, in classic Marx Brothers fashion.

*Funniest Scenes:* The most memorable comedy scene is Chico's "Tutsi-Frutsi ice cream" routine, in which he attempts to sell Groucho racetrack tips. By the time he finally sells Groucho tip sheets, books and guides, the race is already over. There is another laugh-a-minute sequence where red hot blonde floozy Flo attempts to get the best of Dr Hackenbush by seducing him. However when Chico and Harpo show up, they end up driving her nuts. To cure Margaret Dumont of her ailment, Groucho wants to do an examination with Harpo and Chico as assistants. However, they treat Dumont like an automobile at the garage. Harpo's doctor's operating room outfit says 'Joe's Service Station' on the back, and Chico's says 'Brakes Relined.'

*Verdict:* Another hit. Together with *A Night At The Opera, A Day At The Races* is a comedy classic. The performances are winning all the way around, and it is a brilliantly entertaining masterpiece of humour. 4/5

According to Groucho, at this point in his career, he was growing tired of the movie business. He was later to state, 'After Thalberg's death, my interest in the movies waned. I continued to appear in them but my heart was in the Highlands. The fun had gone out of picture making. I was like an old pug, still going through the motions, but now doing it solely for the money.' (1)

Meanwhile, what had happened to Gummo? For a time, he had gone into the ladies garment business in New York City. After that, he became a theatrical agent and his clients included Lana Turner, Barbara Stanwyck, Robert Taylor and Glenn Ford. As for Zeppo, he became an agent like Gummo.

With Irving Thalberg no longer at MGM to personally watch out for The Marx Brothers, they became frustrated in their search for new film projects. It was Zeppo who came up with what sounded like the perfect film for his three brothers. In 1937, George Abbott produced a play on Broadway called *Room Service*. It was about a team of producers who were struggling to put on a show in the face of financial difficulties. Since the play was a hit when it ran in New York, it seemed like a natural choice for The Marx Brothers. Besides, it would represent a break from their usual cinematic personas, and allow them to play slightly different characters. There was no harp solo in it, no Margaret Dumont and a minimum of slapstick bits. However, there was the requisite amount of lunacy already built into the plot. Their friend Morrie Ryskind was brought in to adapt it to the screen for Groucho, Harpo and Chico.

# Room Service (1938)

*The Crew:* William Seiter (Director), George Abbott (Producer), Pandro S Berman (Producer), Morris Ryskind (Screenwriter), Roy Hunt (Cinematographer), George Crone (Editor), Albert Herman (Art Director), Alfred H Herman (Art Director), Van Nest Polglase (Art Director), Roy Webb (Musical Direction/Supervision), Darrell Silvera (Set Designer), Renie (Costume Designer).

*The Cast:* Groucho Marx (Gordon Miller), Chico Marx (Harry Binelli), Harpo Marx (Faker Englund), Lucille Ball (Christine Marlowe), Ann Miller (Hilda Manney), Frank Albertson (Leo Davis), Donald MacBride (Gregory Wagner), Philip Loeb (Timothy Hogarth), Philip Wood (Simon Jenkins), Alexander Asro (Sasha Smirnoff), Charles Halton (Dr Glass), Clifford Dunstan (Joseph Gribble). 78 minutes

*The Story:* Small-time theatre producer Gordon Miller is having trouble financing his new production, which is called *Hail And Farewell*. He has put up the whole cast and crew in the Great White Way Hotel, which just so happens to be managed by his brother-in-law, Joseph Gribble. The director of the production is Harry Binelli, and Miller's business manager is Faker Englund. When a hotel inspector named Wagner tries to evict the whole cast from the hotel, a potential investor shows up to save the day. However there is one complication after another. One complication is the sudden arrival of *Hail And Farewell*'s scriptwriter, Leo Davis. He thinks he is about to make a fortune on his play, but is disillusioned when he finds that there is a major cash flow problem between now and the curtain finally going up on his creation. When everyone loses their accommodation, Harry, Faker and Leo all have to move in with him. They are assisted by two of the cast members: young and innocent Hilda Manney and hard-boiled Christine Marlowe. By the end of the picture, in great show-business tradition, the play finally has its opening night. There are no harp solos for Harpo, and no piano solos for Chico, and no Margaret Dumont. However, it is fun to see the brothers Marx playing characters outside their typical personas.

*Funniest Scenes:* All three of The Marx Brothers prepare for walking out of the hotel without paying the long-overdue bill by putting on every stitch of Groucho's clothes. Harpo at one point smuggles a live turkey into the room with the intention of cooking it. However, the turkey outsmarts him.

*Behind The Scenes:* RKO Studios purchased the rights to John Murray and Allen Boretz' Broadway hit *Room Service* for a reported $255,000. Their next task was to find the right cast for it. Now a talent agent, Zeppo Marx convinced RKO that this would be perfect for his three brothers. He was able to get them for $250,000. At last Zeppo was back in the picture, this time behind the scenes. Although they were still signed to MGM, they were loaned out to RKO to make this film.

*Verdict:* The brothers were looking for a new direction and *Room Service* gave it to them. Although there are no harp solos, or piano solos, this mainly dialogue-driven film still has a lot of laughs in it. It is also fun to see Lucille Ball get in on the Marx insanity, long before *I Love Lucy* made her a television superstar. The film was released on September 21, 1938. Although it did not become a huge hit, it showed that all three brothers were capable of portraying characters slightly different than those they had established on Broadway in the 1920s. 2/5

## *At The Circus (1939)*

*The Crew:* Edward N Buzzell (Director), Mervyn LeRoy (Producer), Irving Brecher (Screenwriter), Leonard Smith (Cinematographer), Harold Arlen (Composer Music Score), EY Harburg (Lyrics), Franz Waxman (Composer Music Score/Musical Direction/Supervision), William Terhune (Editor), Cedric Gibbons (Art Director), Stanley Rogers (Art Director), Edwin B Willis (Set Designer), Dolly Tree (Costume Designer), Bobby Connolly (Choreography).

*The Cast:* Groucho Marx (J Cheever Loophole), Chico Marx (Antonio Pirelli), Harpo Marx (Punchy), Margaret Dumont (Mrs Dukesbury), Florence Rice (Julie Randall), Kenny Baker (Jeff Wilson), Eve Arden (Peerless Pauline), Nat Pendleton (Goliath), Fritz Feld (Jardinet), James Burke (John Carter), Jerry Marenghi (Little Professor Atom), Barnett Parker (Whitcomb). 87 minutes

*The Story:* Jeff Wilson is about to lose the circus he owns, because he is being swindled by Carter, an evil creditor. Jeff's buddy, circus roustabout Antonio, decides that they need the help of a good lawyer, so he hires one named J Cheever Loophole. They are further assisted by circus mascot, Punchy. On board the circus train, someone has stolen the payroll, and Punchy and Antonio try to solve the crime. The musical numbers are a lot of fun in this film. Groucho's turn is a production number called 'Lydia The Tattooed Lady,' and Chico does his trademark piano solo. At one of the towns the circus stops at, Harpo serenades wild lions with an oboe lullaby, which erupts into a swinging soul musical number with an all-Black ensemble. Harpo is irresistibly charming in this jazzy interracial number, which evolves into his requisite harp solo. While other 1930s films were featuring Black performers as either servants or in minstrel numbers, The Marx Brothers were depicting them as friends, co-workers and music partners. The whole show turns into bedlam as the villains let a crazed gorilla loose in the Big Top. Harpo and the gorilla end up on the high wire. Ultimately The Marx Brothers foil the thieves and save the circus.

*Funniest Scenes:* Margaret Dumont getting shot out of a cannon mid-circus is a sheer riot. An extremely game Groucho gives the song, 'Lydia The Tattooed Lady' the kind of insane showmanship that it needs - making this his best musical number. Hard-boiled dame, Eve Arden, is hysterical as she verbally spars with Groucho, then tries to romance him while simultaneously picking his pocket. Eve and Groucho's best bit comes when she talks him into wearing anti-gravity shoes like the ones she wears in her act. Chico and Harpo get the biggest laughs when they sneak into the train compartment of the evil strong man Goliath and attempt to not wake him up while they search for the stolen money. Also, Groucho operating a button hook, in a strained effort to fasten Margaret Dumont's dress.

*Behind The Scenes:* This was the first Marx Brothers film for MGM with Irving Thalberg totally absent from the proceedings. Because of this, there was no out-of-town stage rehearsal of the comedy routines. Silent-film star Buster Keaton was brought in to come up with gags for Harpo. It was released on October 20, 1939.

*Verdict:* Although Marxian purists claim that this film represented a slackening in The Marx Brothers' comedy panache, *At The Circus* still contains several laughs. 4/5

Irving Thalberg had put forward the idea for a western picture for The Marx Brothers, so that's what they did next. It was agreed that there was a flatness to the last two films, so MGM agreed to finance a stage tour to work out some of the gags for *Go West*. Appearing in both Chicago and Detroit, The Marx Brothers logged 103 performances, which gave them enough time to polish the jokes in front of a live audience - which was always their strong point.

## *Go West (1940)*

*The Crew:* Edward N Buzzell (Director), Jack Cummings (Producer), Irving Brecher (Screenwriter), Leonard Smith (Cinematographer), George Bassman (Composer Music Score), Roger Edens (Composer Music Score), Blanche Sewell (Editor), Cedric Gibbons (Art Director), Stanley Rogers (Art Director), George Stoll (Musical Direction/Supervision), Edwin B Willis (Set Designer).

*The Cast:* Groucho Marx (S Quentin Quayle), Harpo Marx (Rusty Panello), Chico Marx (Joseph Panello), John Carroll (Terry Turner), Diana Lewis (Eve Wilson), Walter Woolf King (Mr Beecher), Robert H Barrat (Red Baxter), June MacCloy (Lulubelle), George Lessey (Railroad President), Iris Adrian (Saloon Girl), Joan Woodbury (Saloon Girl), Clem Bevans (Official), Arthur Houseman (Drunk), Mitchell Lewis (Halfbreed), Tully Marshall (Dan Wilson), Joe Yule (Bartender). 81 minutes

*The Story:* It is 1870 and S Quentin Quayle is trying to scrape together his train fare to head West. Running into two rubes, Rusty and Joe, he thinks he is going to swindle them in a card game. However, they end up swindling him. Somehow, they all end up out West and get embroiled in a land-owning scheme. When a railroad company is torn between two plots of land, the owners of each piece of property are in direct competition for the railroad to write a check for them. The bad guys, Beecher and Baxter, plot to pull the railroad deal from the film's hero, Terry Turner. Idiots that they are, Rusty and Joe write an IOU note for beer at the saloon on the back of the much sought-after land deed. United in their goal to save the deed for Eve Wilson and her grandfather, The Marx Brothers go head to head with the villains and the conniving dance-hall girls. The finale is a battle to control a moving train, with Groucho, Chico and Harpo winning the battle, at the cost of destroying the entire train, passenger cars and all.

*Funniest Scenes: Go West* was released on December 6, 1940. Although it only did so-so business at the box office, like all of their films it contained several genuine laughs. The opening sequence between Groucho, Harpo and Chico, where they are trying to swindle each other, is a riot. Harpo has his harp solo in the local Indian village, using the strings of a rug weaving loom to play his song for the tribe. Also, the scene where the dance-hall girls try to get Groucho, Chico and Harpo drunk, is very funny.

At one point in the film, Groucho gets into a stagecoach with Chico and Harpo already aboard. Also in the coach are a man and two women. One of the women is carrying a crying baby. While the coach is pitching and bouncing due to the rough terrain, Groucho turns to the woman with the infant and asks, "Madame, why is that baby constantly crying?" The woman replies, "He can't stand the 'jerks' in the coach." With that, Chico and Harpo stand up and head for the door.

In another scene, Groucho confuses the chief of an Indian tribe for the Super Chief passenger train. Meeting the Native American tribe leader, Groucho inquires, "Are you the chief that runs from Chicago to Los Angeles in 39 hours?"

The Buster Keaton-inspired finale (taken from Keaton's masterpiece *The General*) involved The Marx Brothers being at the helm of a runaway passenger train. When they run out of wood to fuel the train, they begin breaking up the railroad cars to beat the villains to their destination.

*Behind The Scenes:* There were plans for The Marx Brothers' *Go West* on the drawing boards back in 1936, personally overseen by Irving Thalberg. At that time Irving had enlisted Bert Kalmar and Harry Ruby to concoct a Marx Brothers' feature involving a rodeo. *Go West* ended up put on hold and *A Day At The Races* went into production instead.

*Verdict:* Although many critics find *Go West* lacking in the middle, this film contains some riotous funny scenes in it. Along with *At The Circus*, *Go West* is often overlooked, and unfairly so. The plot to this film is paper thin, but the ridiculous routines of The Marx Brothers make this entertaining throughout. 4/5

## *The Big Store (1941)*

*The Crew:* Charles "Chuck" Riesner (Director), Louis K Sidney (Producer), Hal Fimberg (Screenwriter/Songwriter), Ray Golden (Screenwriter/Songwriter), Sid Kuller (Screenwriter/Songwriter), Charles Lawton (Cinematographer), George Bassman (Composer Music Score), Hal Borne (Composer Music Score)/Songwriter), George Stoll (Composer Music Score/Musical Direction/Supervision), Conrad A Nervig (Editor), Cedric Gibbons (Art Director), Stanley Rogers (Art Director), Milton Drake (Songwriter), Ben Oakland (Songwriter), Artie Shaw & His Band (Songwriter), Edwin B Willis (Set Designer), Arthur Appel (Choreography), Douglas Shearer (Sound/Sound Designer).

*The Cast:* Groucho Marx (Wolf J Flywheel), Chico Marx (Ravelli), Harpo Marx (Wacky), Tony Martin (Tommy Rogers), Virginia Grey (Joan Sutton), Margaret Dumont (Martha Phelps), Douglas Dumbrille (Mr Grover), William Tannen (Fred Sutton), Marion Martin (Peggy Arden), Virginia O'Brien (Kitty), Henry Armetta (Giuseppe), Anna Demetrio (Maria), Paul Stanton (George Hastings), Russell Hicks (Arthur Hastings), Bradley Page (Duke). 80 minutes

*The Story:* Martha Phelps is the owner of Phelps, a major department store, and her sole heir is singer Tommy Rogers. There is a plot underfoot to get Tommy out of the picture and take over the control of the store. Martha decides to hire detective Wolf J Flywheel to be Tommy's bodyguard. She doesn't realise that while she is being courted by Grover, she is being set up by him. Grover has plans to marry Martha and do away with both she and her nephew. Flywheel's trusty assistant is a man named Wacky. Tommy's main ally is his pal, Ravelli, a piano teacher. Grover attempts to have Tommy killed, but his plans fail. He later plans to kidnap Tommy's girlfriend, Joan. Groucho gets his swingingest musical number ever on 'Sing While You Shop.' Harpo gets his lushest harp number, when he stumbles into a Louis XIV display at the store, and has a fantasy sequence, where three Harpos in period clothing perform as a trio. Naturally, by the end of the picture The Marx Brothers, in their own bumbling way, defeat the villains.

*Funniest Scenes:* The very best scene is the one with Harpo and Groucho in Flywheel's office trying to make breakfast. With a stove top that opens out of a desk, a hen in a cage to lay eggs and several foldaway devices, this scene is a panic. Even a Murphy bed folds into the wall to mimic legal file cabinets when a client arrives. Harpo serves as assistant and short-order cook in this silly sequence. Harpo has another very funny scene, when a haughty customer demands of a salesgirl a swatch of fabric to match her dress. Harpo goes behind her, cuts the back of the woman's skirt off while she stands there, and presents it to her. Another crazy scene unfolds with all three Marx Brothers in the bed department of Phelps. Several multi-ethnic families displace their children when Harpo starts pulling levers, and five-story bunk beds and other crazy thematic beds begin to fold in and out of walls and the floor.

*Behind The Scenes:* Just after filming had finished on *The Big Store*, Groucho, Chico and Harpo decided to officially disband. The announcement came in April 1941, and they even used it as a selling point in the preview trailer for *The Big Store*. It showed The Marx Brothers through a open window (cut to stock footage of a cheering crowd down below), with Groucho announcing: "We didn't know you cared. But, since you do, we'll present to you songs and scenes from our first farewell picture, *The Big Store*." With that, Chico says, "Where everything's a good buy." Then Groucho bids the crowd, "Goodbye."

*Verdict:* The plot here wears a bit thin, but The Marx Brothers' films were never terribly plot driven. It's the gags that make this film enjoyable. Instead of relying on Groucho, Harpo and Chico's jokes to propel the undoing of the crooks, special-effects shots fill this with more physical comedy. In spite of its flaws, there are still several great routines in *The Big Store*. 2/5

It was "Goodbye" to The Marx Brothers for a while. However, they were clearly just waiting for someone to beg them to come back. On June 15, 1942, Groucho and Ruth Marx divorced. On March 27, 1943, Groucho returned to the radio airwaves, this time as the star of *Pabst Blue Ribbon Town*, presented by Pabst Blue Ribbon Beer. On July 21, 1945, Groucho married his second wife, Kay Gorcey. In the meanwhile, Chico started his own jazz band, with whom he toured, coming out on stage to perform his trademark acrobatic piano solos mid-show. Harpo became something of a family man. Since his wife, Susan, was unable to have children, they began adopting their own Marx clan, which eventually included Bill, Alexander, James, Arthur and Minnie.

Harpo was to keep in touch with many of his lifelong friends. When George S Kaufman wrote his most popular play, with Moss Hart, *The Man Who Came To Dinner*, one of the characters, Banjo, was inspired by Harpo. In the film version, Banjo was played by Jimmy Durante. In July 1941, at Buck's County Playhouse, Harpo appeared as Banjo, with Moss Hart as Beverly Carlton, and George S Kaufman as Whiteside - the man who came to dinner and would never leave.

Over the next few years, whilst America was involved in World War II, both Groucho and Harpo promoted the sale of war bonds. When the war was almost finished, The Marx Brothers were invited back from their self-imposed retirement.

One of the most popular films of the war years was the 1942 epic *Casablanca*, starring Humphrey Bogart and Ingrid Bergman. Someone had the inspired idea of taking The Marx Brothers, landing them in post-war Casablanca and letting them drive

Nazi war criminals out of their minds. When the idea of returning to movie-making came to mind, there were several reasons for such a venture. Firstly, Groucho was getting bored with his radio performances. Secondly, Chico really needed the money.

## *A Night In Casablanca (1946)*

*The Crew:* Archie Mayo (Director), David L Loew (Producer), Joseph Fields (Screenwriter), Roland Kibbee (Screenwriter), Frank Tashlin (Screenwriter), James Van Trees (Cinematographer), Werner Janssen (Composer Music Score), Duncan Cramer (Production Designer), Bert Kalmar (Songwriter), Harry Ruby (Songwriter), Ted Snyder (Songwriter), Edward Boyle (Set Designer), Otis Malcolm (Make-up), Jack Sullivan (First Assistant Director), Frank Webster (Sound/Sound Designer).

*The Cast:* Groucho Marx (Ronald Kornblow), Harpo Marx (Rusty), Chico Marx (Corbaccio), Lisette Verea (Béatrice Rheiner), Charlie Drake (Lt. Pierre Delmar), Lois Collier (Annette), Dan Seymour (Captain Brizzard), Lewis L Russell (Governor Galoux), Frederick Giermann (Kurt), Sig Rumann (Count Pfefferman alias Heinrich Stubel), Paul Harvey (Mr Smythe), David Hoffman (Spy), Harro Meller (Emil), Ruth Roman (Bit Part). 85 minutes

*The Story:* Somehow the managers of the Hotel Casablanca are ending up murdered. The newest manager is a bumbling idiot named Ronald Kornblow, who is oblivious to the danger he is in by holding this post. There also seems to be a fortune in Nazi-confiscated loot hidden somewhere in the area. Escaped Nazi war criminal Heinrich Stubel is apparently behind it. He is assisted by a valet named Rusty, to whom he is abusive. The town is filled with questionable characters, and bumbling ones like Corbaccio, who is the owner of the Yellow Camel Cab Company. He becomes Kornblow's personal bodyguard. Unable to rub out Kornblow himself, Stubel enlists femme fatale Béatrice Rheiner to seduce Kornblow. Framed on trumped-up charges, Kornblow, Corbaccio and Rusty escape just in time to defeat Stubel and his cohorts.

*Funniest Scenes:* Near the beginning, Harpo is seen leaning against a wall. He is asked, "Say, what do you think you're doing? Holding up the building?" With that Harpo nods affirmatively. "Come on," he is commanded. Once he is no longer leaning against the building, it collapses into a pile of rubble.

At one point in the film Groucho is sparring with femme fatale Béatrice. When she says to him, "I shall be in the supper club tonight. Will you join me?", Groucho fires back at her, "Why? Are you coming apart?" Another time they are trying to outdo each other with tobacco smoke. When the smoke clears Groucho says, "This is like living in Pittsburgh - if you can call that a living!"

There is an insanely funny scene in which The Marx Brothers sneak into the room of the villain, and play switcharoo with luggage.

*Behind The Scenes:* This was originally going to be a direct parody of *Casablanca*, with characters set to be called Humphrey Bogus instead of Humphrey Bogart and Lowen Behold instead of Lauren Bacall.

When The Marx Brothers announced that their next picture would be called *A Night In Casablanca*, Warner Brothers Pictures staked claim to the name 'Casablanca.' To answer such an absurd assumption, Groucho fired back the first in a series of famous letters to Warner Brothers. The first one, addressed to the Warner Brothers legal department read in part: 'I am sure that the average movie fan could learn in time to distinguish between Ingrid Bergman and Harpo. I don't know whether I could, but I certainly would like to try. You claim you own 'Casablanca' and that no one else can use that name without your permission. What about 'Warner Brothers?' Do you own that, too? You probably have the right to use the name Warner, but what about 'Brothers?' Professionally, we were brothers long before you were. We were touring the sticks as The Marx Brothers when Vitaphone was still a gleam in the inventor's eye.' (30)

One of the most attractive aspects of filming *A Night In Casablanca* was the fact that a budget was approved for a pre-filming theatre tour. The original running length was two hours but after a preview screening proved less than satisfactory, the film was trimmed down by 30 minutes.

Finally, after the longest gap between any of their films, *A Night In Casablanca* opened on May 10, 1946. Although brilliantly conceived as a spoof on the Bogart/Bergman film, this was not the box-office hit that Groucho had hoped.

*Verdict: A Night In Casablanca* has funny bits but it loses steam mid-way through the film. 3/5


In spite of the windfall pay cheque he received for appearing in *A Night In Casablanca*, Chico was still having money troubles.

On August 14, 1946, Groucho and Kay's daughter, Melinda, was born. Groucho was already at work on his first solo film project away from his famous brothers. *Copacabana* was a musical starring him and the South American bombshell, Carmen Miranda. While *Copacabana* was in production in late 1946, Groucho had written his daughter Miriam a letter in which he informed her that he had just screened one of Miranda's films. In the letter he summed up Carmen Miranda by writing, 'In addition to looking like a dressed-up bulldog, she sings each song the same as the preceding one, and to top it off, she is supposed to feed me [lines of dialogue] in the picture, and I didn't understand a God-damned word she uttered!' (31) *Copacabana* opened on May 30, 1947. It was less than successful creatively.

On October 27, 1947, Groucho Marx made his initial appearance as the star and host of the radio program *You Bet Your Life* for the ABC Radio Network. This particular show, and its subsequent television incarnation, was to represent a second career for Groucho.

In 1949, the final Marx Brothers' movie went into production. *Love Happy* was originally a vehicle for Harpo Marx – it was based on his idea. However, it experienced budget problems mid-production, and to bolster its box-office potential, Harpo first talked Chico, then Groucho into participating in the project.

## *Love Happy (1949)*

*The Crew:* David Miller (Director), Lester Cowan (Producer), Mary Pickford (Producer), Mac Benoff (Screenwriter), Frank Tashlin (Screenwriter), William Mellor (Cinematographer), Ann Ronell (Composer Music Score), Al Joseph (Editor), Basil Wrangell (Editor), Gabriel Scognamillo (Production Designer), Paul J Smith (Musical Direction/ Supervision), Casey Roberts (Set Designer), Grace Houston (Costume Designer), Norma (Costume Designer), Billy Daniel (Choreography), Fred Phillips (Make-up), Howard A Anderson (Special Effects).

*The Cast:* Groucho Marx (Detective Sam Grunion), Harpo Marx (Harpo), Chico Marx (Faustino The Great), Ilona Massey (Madame Egelichi), Vera-Ellen (Maggie Phillips), Raymond Burr (Alphonse Zoto), Marion Hutton (Bunny Dolan), Bruce Gordon (Hannibal Zoto), Melville Cooper (Throckmorton), Leon Belasco (Mr Lyons), Paul Valentine (Mike Johnson), Eric Blore (Mackinaw), Marilyn Monroe (Grunion's Client). 91 minutes

*The Story: Love Happy* is similar in storyline to *Room Service*, in that the central theme of the movie is about a group of struggling actors attempting to put on a show in New York City, but lack cash. This time around, a clown named Harpo is the central character. He is the mascot/guardian angel to the troupe of actors. They rely upon him to shoplift food to feed them until they can get the show off the ground. The group of actors includes a shapely actress/dancer named Maggie Phillips, and a brassy singer named Bunny Dolan. When Harpo fills his pockets with food for his troupe of actors, he inadvertently lifts a special can of sardines from a gourmet food shop. The can contains hidden treasure - a stolen diamond necklace of the Romanov family. The femme fatale this time around is vampy Madame Egelichi, who has the ability to hypnotise people with her famed double whammy of a spell. Her henchmen include Alphonse Zoto. Harpo's buddy is pianist Faustino The Great, who naturally fits in a couple of piano numbers in the film. A private eye named Sam Grunion is not only the narrator of the film, but is also trying to solve the case of the missing diamonds. For the only time in a Marx Brothers' film, Groucho is seen without his trademark painted-on moustache.

Vera-Ellen has a great dance number and Marion Hutton sings an amusing comedy song called 'Mama Wants To Know' - sung in the fashion of her movie star sister Betty Hutton.

*Funniest Scenes:* Harpo is amusing to watch while being hypnotised by femme fatale Ilona Massey. Harpo's gallop amidst the neon signs of Times Square is good for laughs, especially his ride on the red-winged horse trademark of Mobil Oil. Chico manages to get entangled in the plot when the diamond necklace ends up in the strings of his grand piano - mid-performance. He has some amusing comedy bits, including his famous dialogue with one of the play's producers: "You know *allegro pizzicato*?" "No," replies the producer. "You know Jimmy Pizzicato?" asks Chico. The most famous scene from *Love Happy* remains the one minute in the picture when then-starlet Marilyn Monroe walks into detective Groucho Marx's office to announce, "Some men are following me." Not missing a beat, Groucho replies, "Really? I can't imagine why."

*Behind The Scenes:* One of the most interesting aspects of *Love Happy* is the fact that it was one of the first films to openly feature something that is now seen as commonplace in the 21st Century - product placement in a theatrical film release. In *Love*

*Happy*, Harpo has a rooftop chase scene segment, where he is seen comically being pursued amidst the giant neon signs of Times Square of New York City. Among the giant neon signs he is seen against are conspicuous logos for Kool Cigarettes and its trademark penguin, Mobil Oil's famed red flying horse, and Bulova Watches. The reason for this was that United Artists withdrew their funding and the production was running low on money. The film's producer, Lester Cowen, very resourcefully went to the advertising departments of each of these products, and openly solicited paid advertising just to get the movie completed.

Although Love Happy was filmed and copyrighted in 1949, further financial problems delayed the opening of the film until March 3, 1950.

*Verdict:* Compared to the high points of hilarity of the best of The Marx Brothers' films, *Love Happy* is a bit flat and half-baked. However, what remains is a charming but slightly silly story about struggling actors trying to put on a show. The minute-long Marilyn Monroe cameo is very cute, and it is a treat to see her as a brunette and not a bleached blonde sex goddess. While it is a shame that the final Marx Brothers' film isn't a lunatic blockbuster, it is still fun to see them still mugging for the movie cameras 20 years past their screen debut in *The Cocoanuts*. 1/5

# 8. The TV And Radio Years

On May 12, 1950, Groucho and Kay Marx were divorced. Two months later, on July 17, 1950, Groucho made his television debut on the CBS-TV program, *The Popsicle Parade Of Stars*. After years of dabbling in radio, he was to find a new career in television. It was on October 5, 1950, that Groucho marked his first television broadcast of *You Bet Your Life*, which was shown on NBC-TV. During his eleven-year run on television with *You Bet Your Life*, Groucho also made solo guest appearances in movies. The first such cameo came on December 20, 1950, when *Mr Music* opened. It was a Bing Crosby movie, in which Crosby plays a songwriter who is living far beyond the constraints of his income, and featured several guest appearances, including Groucho. This was to be the pattern for much of the rest of Groucho's film career. Even after thirteen Marx Brothers films, he rarely was cast in movies except as a special guest star.

On January 23, 1951, Groucho won an Emmy Award as The Most Outstanding Television Personality Of 1950. Although the television version of *You Bet Your Life* was only months old, he had already become a welcome fixture on millions of American television screens every week.

In rapid succession, Groucho managed to star in two films from this era. The first one was called *Double Dynamite*, which opened on December 24, 1951. Co-starring Frank Sinatra and Jane Russell, it was the tale of a bank teller who accidentally saves a gangster's life. On January 23, 1952, the Groucho Marx/William Bendix film, *A Girl In Every Port* opened. It was about a couple of sailors who smuggle a race horse onto a ship. Neither film made much noise at the box office.

In October 1952, Groucho Marx was in the record stores, having just released his first full-length LP: *Hooray For Captain Spaulding And Other Songs By Harry Ruby And Bert Kilmar Sung By Groucho Marx*. It was released by Decca Records.

It was on July 17, 1954, that Groucho Marx married his third wife, Eden Hartford.

On July 26, 1957, the first major Jayne Mansfield movie, *Will Success Spoil Rock Hunter?*, opened. Groucho Marx was one of the hit film's guest stars.

In the late 1950s Groucho, Harpo and Chico were reunited for three separate projects. In October 8, 1957, the film *The Story Of Mankind* was released, featuring Groucho, Harpo, and Chico Marx. However, none of the brothers were in the others' scenes. This was to be the last motion picture in which all three of them appeared.

On March 8, 1959, Groucho, Harpo and Chico made their final television appearance together in an episode of TV's *GE Theatre* entitled *The Incredible Jewel Robbery*. Essentially, at the end of a scene between Chico and Harpo, Groucho made an unbilled walk-on.

Also in 1959, The Marx Brothers filmed a TV pilot for a series of their own, in which they appeared as angels, with Groucho in the scene making witty comments. It was called *The Deputy Seraph*. Unfortunately, after it was filmed, the show idea was abandoned, and it disappeared from sight for several years. In September 1959, Groucho Marx published his first autobiography, *Groucho And Me*.

It was on September 21, 1961 that Groucho was seen on the final broadcast of his long-running television show, *You Bet Your Life*. It had been a great run for him, and gave him a wonderful third career - following theatre and movies. He had been a bona fide multimedia star for nearly 50 years - one of the longest careers in show-business history. If one takes into account the fact that he began in vaudeville, graduated to Broadway, blossomed in films, segued into radio and had made the transition into television, few performers enjoyed the career longevity that Groucho Marx continued to enjoy. He had even branched off into record albums and books!

On October 11, 1961, only weeks after Groucho's *You Bet Your Life* went off the air, Chico Marx died. It was the end of an era. The Marx Brothers would publicly perform together no more.

However, on television, Groucho would continue to work through the 1960s. On January 11, 1962, he was back on television on his new CBS-TV show, *Tell It To Groucho*. Groucho's next book, *Memoirs Of A Mangy Lover*, was published and hit the stores in October 1963.

On April 24, 1964, Groucho Marx was seen as the star of the television drama, *Time For Elizabeth* on NBC-TV's *Bob Hope Chrysler Theatre*. And, on September 28, 1964, Harpo Marx died.

In June 1965, the television show *Groucho* premiered in Great Britain on BBC-TV. It was the British version of *You Bet Your Life*. And, in February 1967, Simon & Schuster Publishers released *The Groucho Letters*, a compilation of letters to and from Groucho Marx throughout the years.

On December 19, 1968, the film with the final Groucho Marx guest appearance, *Skidoo*, was released. It was an Otto Preminger-directed Jackie Gleason comedy.

December 4, 1969, saw the divorce of Groucho and Eden Marx.

In the fall of 1971, a book compiled by Darien House, including an introduction penned by Groucho Marx, entitled *Why A Duck?*, was published. It consisted of film stills from all of The

Marx Brothers' films, and snippets of on-screen dialogue and gag lines. It was edited by avid Marx Brothers' fan, Richard J Anobile. Groucho wrote a rambling introduction to the book, which, while it had little to do with introducing the material on the successive pages of the book, still had the same Groucho wit that he was famous for. At one point he pointed out, "You probably noticed that in a previous paragraph, I said 'bastards' instead of 'What the heck' or 'In a pig's eye!' It's my way of trying to keep up with this changing world. To tell you the truth, I haven't done too well at it. When the Sexual Revolution began, I tried to enlist. But all I got was a series of humiliating rejections." (32)

On May 6, 1972, Groucho Marx was back on stage, at New York City's Carnegie Hall no less! It was a one-night-only affair and a memorable one by all reports. Groucho, at his cantankerous best reminisced, told jokes and proved once and for all, what a trooper he was. The evening was recorded for posterity and was eventually released as a record album.

Groucho Marx and Richard J Anobile had such great success with the publication of *Why A Duck?* that they reunited to produce *The Marx Brothers' Scrapbook.* Based on his interviews with Groucho and other key Marx figures, the book was published originally by Darien House, and hit the stores in October 1973.

On April 2, 1974, Groucho Marx was honoured publicly by his peers, as he accepted an honorary Academy Award. He accepted the award on behalf of himself and his brothers.

On January 16, 1977, The Four Marx Brothers were inducted into the Motion Picture Hall Of Fame. Both Groucho and his brother Zeppo were present at the ceremony, which was held at the Wilshire Hyatt House Hotel in Hollywood. It was to be Groucho's final public appearance.

In rapid succession, the remaining of The Marx Brothers passed away. When Gummo died on April 21, 1977, Groucho was in such frail health that a decision was made by his relatives not to inform him. Less than four months later, on August 19, 1977, Groucho died. Then, on November 29, 1979, Zeppo passed away.

Their legacy has been recognised since then. In 1990 the American Library of Congress added *Duck Soup* to the US National Film Registry, as a cinematic treasure. In 1998, the American Film Institute tallied their choices of the 100 Greatest American Movies of all times and *Duck Soup* was on the official list. Their work is available on video and DVD for people to enjoy in the comfort of their own homes.

Although the lives of The Marx Brothers are over, thanks to their films, their zany sense of humour and their genius as comedians live on to this day.

# 9. Obscure Marx Films And Shorts

This is a list of lesser-known screen appearances by The Marx Brothers, including their long-missing unreleased silent film, their short subject films, as well as films in which individual Marx Brothers appeared separately from their siblings.

*Humour Risk* (1922) - This is The Marx Brothers' long-lost self-produced silent film. It received one known screening and was a dismal failure. The negative was presented to the members of the Algonquin Round Table in the mid-1920s, and has never shown up since.

*Too Many Kisses* (1925) - Harpo Marx is seen in this silent film starring Richard Dix, Frances Howard and William Powell. Lost for years, a copy turned up in the 1990s, and scenes can be seen on the commercially available documentary *The Unknown Marx Brothers*.

*The House That Shadows Built* (1931) - Groucho, Chico, Harpo and Zeppo recreate their agent's office sequence from their show *On The Mezzanine*.

*Hollywood On Parade* (1932) - A promotional one-reel film featuring Groucho, Harpo and Chico.

*Hollywood On Parade* (1933) - Another promotional one-reel film, featuring Chico Marx as well as WC Fields.

*La Fiesta De Santa Barbara* (1935) - A promotional short film which includes Harpo Marx and The Gumm Sisters - including Judy (Gumm) Garland.

*Yours For The Asking* (1936) - A George Raft and Ida Lupino film, in which Groucho Marx can be spotted as an extra in one of the scenes.

*Hollywood - The Second Step* (1936) - A short promotional film including Chico Marx and Maureen Sullivan.

*Sunday Night At The Trocadero* (1937) - A short promotional film at the Hollywood nightspot, featuring Mr & Mrs Groucho Marx and Robert Benchley.

*Screen Snapshots Number Two* (1943) - A one-reel short featuring Groucho Marx and Carole Landis.

*Screen Door Canteen* (1943) - A wartime picture with everyone in Hollywood making a cameo appearance, including Harpo Marx.

*Screen Snapshots Number 8* (1943) - A one-reel short featuring Groucho, Harpo and Chico, as well as Gene Autry and Tyrone Power.

*The All-Star Band Rally* (1945) - A two-reel short film including Bing Crosby, Betty Grable, Carmen Miranda and Harpo Marx.

*Copacabana* (1947) - Groucho Marx and Carmen Miranda in their own starring role feature. This movie is so dreadful it makes *Love Happy* look like *Gone With The Wind*.

*Mr Music* (1950) - A Bing Crosby film with Groucho Marx in a guest appearance.

*Double Dynamite* (1951) - Starring Frank Sinatra, Groucho Marx and Jane Russell in a tale about a bank teller accidentally saving the life of a gangster.

*A Girl In Every Port* (1952) - Groucho Marx and William Bendix attempt to smuggle a race horse onto a passenger ship.

*Will Success Spoil Rock Hunter?* (1957) - Finally solo Groucho Marx in a major motion picture - alas in a cameo role. Jayne Mansfield, Tony Randall, Tony Curtis and Joan Blondell star in this spoof about the early days of television.

*The Story Of Mankind* (1957) - Groucho, Harpo and Chico all have cameo roles in this Ronald Coleman and Vincent Price film. Groucho plays Peter Minuit, Harpo is Isaac Newton and Chico plays a monk. However, they are never on screen together.

*Skidoo* (1968) - A film starring Jackie Gleason and Carol Channing. Groucho Marx is in a featured role, as God.

# 10. Marx Brothers On Video And DVD

## Films

*The Cocoanuts* (1929) Video & DVD

*Animal Crackers* (1930) Video & DVD

*Monkey Business* (1931) Video & DVD

*Horse Feathers* (1932) Video & DVD

*Duck Soup* (1933) Video & DVD

*A Night At The Opera* (1935) Video

*A Day At The Races* (1937) Video

*Room Service* (1938) Video

*At The Circus* (1939) Video

*Go West* (1940) Video

*The Big Store* (1941) Video

*A Night In Casablanca* (1946) Video

*Love Happy* (1949) Video

## Documentary

*The Unknown Marx Brothers* (1993) Video & DVD

Leslie Nielsen narrates this excellent overview of The Marx Brothers' careers, from vaudeville to their television appearances. It includes rare filmed footage like scenes of Harpo Marx in the newly discovered silent film *Too Many Kisses* (1925), the agent's scene from *On The Mezzanine* contained in the rare film short *The House That Shadows Built* (1931), and the very last filmed Marx Brothers' skit from the never-shown TV pilot for *The Deputy Seraph* (1959).

# 11. Quote Sources

(1) *Groucho And Me*, book, by Groucho Marx, Bernard Geis Associates Publishers, 1976.

(2) *The Marx Brothers Scrapbook*, book, by Groucho Marx and Richard J Anobile, Darien House Publishers, 1973.

(3) *The Groucho Phile, An Illustrated Life,* book, by Groucho Marx and Hector Arce, Gallahad Books, 1976.

(4) *The Dallas Morning News*, newspaper, December 25, 1905.

(5) *The San Antonio Light*, newspaper, January 7, 1906.

(6) *Variety*, newspaper, November 30, 1906.

(7) *Liberty*, magazine, by Clara Beranger, June 3, 1933.

(8) *Variety*, newspaper, December 21, 1907.

(9) *Saturday Evening Post*, magazine, 'Bad Days Are Good Memories,' by Groucho Marx, August 29, 1931.

(10) *Harpo Speaks*, book, by Harpo Marx with Rowland Barber, Bernard Geis Associates/Random House Publishers, 1961.

(11) *Variety*, newspaper, February 24, 1912.

(12) *Variety*, newspaper, by Wynn, May 19, 1912.

(13) *The Kalamazoo Gazette*, newspaper, January 13, 1913.

(14) *The Salt Lake Telegram*, newspaper, November 13, 1913.

(15) *Clipper*, newspaper, January 14, 1914.

(16) *The Freedonia Gazette*, newspaper, Winter 1981.

(17) *Variety*, newspaper, full-page ad by Minnie (Marx) Palmer, 1914.

(18) *Variety*, newspaper, September 24, 1914.

(19) *The Los Angeles Times*, newspaper, 'Why Harpo Doesn't Talk,' by Groucho Marx, December 12, 1948.

(20) *The Flint Daily Journal*, newspaper, September 3, 1915.

(21) *Redbook*, magazine, feature, by Groucho Marx, 1933.

(22) *The Times*, newspaper; London, England; June 27, 1922.

(23) *Variety,* newspaper, 'Unit Show with $60 In Box Office, Attached,' March 8, 1923.

(24) *Variety*, newspaper, May 3, 1923.

(25) *Public Ledger*, newspaper; Philadelphia, Pennsylvania; *I'll Say She Is* Has Propitious Opening, June 5, 1923.

(26) *The New York Sun*, newspaper, 'Harpo Marx And Some Brothers: Hilarious Antics Spread Good Cheer At The Casino,' by Alexander Wollcott, May 20, 1924.

(27) *Monkey Business: The Lives And Legends Of The Marx Brothers*, book, by Louvish, Simon, St Martin's Press, 1999.

(28) *Growing Up With Chico*, book, by Maxine Marx, Prentice Hall Publishers, 1980.

(29) *The History Of Movie Comedy*, book, by Janice Anderson, Exeter Books, Simon & Schuster Publishers, 1985.

(30) *The Groucho Letters*, book, by Groucho Marx, Sphere Books, 1969.

(31) *Love, Groucho*, book, by Miriam Marx, Faber & Faber, 1992.

(32) *Why A Duck?*, book, by Groucho Marx and Richard J Anobile, New York Graphic Society, Avon Books, 1973.

# 12. Bibliography

Adamson, Joe, *Groucho, Harpo, Chico And Sometimes Zeppo*, Simon & Schuster, 1973.

Anderson, Janice, *The History Of Movie Comedy*, Exeter Books, Simon & Schuster, 1985.

Bader, Robert S (editor), *Groucho Marx And Other Short Stories And Tall Tales,* Faber & Faber, 1993.

Louvish, Simon, *Monkey Business: The Lives And Legends Of The Marx Brothers*, St Martin's Press, 1999.

Martin, Mick and Porter, Marsha, *Video Movie Guide 2001*, Ballantine Books, 2000.

Marx, Groucho, *Groucho And Me*, Bernard Geis Associates Publishers, 1976.

Marx, Groucho and Anobile, Richard J, *Why A Duck?*, New York Graphic Society, Avon Books, 1973.

Marx, Groucho and Anobile, Richard J, *The Marx Brothers Scrapbook*, Darien House Publishers, 1973.

Marx, Groucho and Arce, Hector, *The Groucho Phile, An Illustrated Life*, Gallahad Books, 1976.

Marx, Harpo with Barber, Rowland, *Harpo Speaks*, Bernard Geis Associates/Random House Publishers, 1961.

Marx, Maxine, *Growing Up With Chico*, Prentice Hall Publishers, 1980.

Monaco, James and The Editors Of Baseline, *The Encyclopaedia Of Film*, Perigee Books, 1991

Quinlan, David, *Quinlan's Illustrated Registry Of Film Stars*, Henry Holt Publishers, 1991

# 13. Websites

More information, photos, trivia and Marx Brothers fun can be found on the Internet. There are several Marx Brothers websites that have been set up by fans of the fabulous five brothers Marx., as listed below. These have all been personally viewed, and were up and running at the time of this book's publication.

## 1. The Marx Brothers
## Four Of The Three Musketeers

A cleverly conceived and executed site with information and photos on Marx books, videos, films, vaudeville, radio and television appearances and performances by all five Marx Brothers. Also, this site features the option of getting the information in the German language as well as English.

Address: http://www.marx-brothers.org/

## 2. The Marx Brothers' Hollywood

This is a good site for anyone visiting Los Angeles, as it lists different spots around the Hollywood area which are key to the Marx Brothers' history, including Margaret Dumont's burial site, Groucho's former Hollywood house, the addresses of studios they once worked at, and some of their hangouts. Note that many of the sites have seriously changed since The Marx Brothers era. For instance, Graumann's Chinese Theater is now called Mann's Chinese Theater, and the once fabulous Chasen's restaurant is now a grocery store.

Address: http://seeing-stars.com/StarIndexes/MarxBros.shtml

### 3. The Inimitable Marx Brothers

A multi-media site, complete with audio sound clips, book reviews, and even downloadable movie posters from the Marx Brothers' movies and Broadway shows.

Address: http://www.marxbros.yucom.be

### 4. Brad's Marx Brothers Page

This site is presented in glorious black & white to preserve the integrity of the Marx Brothers' films. Brad presents news, biographies, film information, web links, photographs, and wav files of five Marx Brothers songs, plus transcripts of song lyrics to 'Lydia The Tattooed Lady' and 'Hooray For Captain Spaulding.'

Address: http://members.tripod.com/Cleo256/marx/

### 5. Why A Duck?

In addition to movie and career information, this mainly black & white site features some unique elements, including astrological birth charts for all five Marx Brothers, and excerpts of various scripts, including the Napoleon scene from *I'll Say She Is*. It also features, games, quizzes and Marx Brothers crossword puzzles.

Address: http://www.whyaduck.com/index.htm

### 6. Marxist Propaganda

A sparse but informative site that features biographical information on the five brothers, as well as film clips including Harpo's mirror scene, and Groucho's dance from *Duck Soup*. There are also links to find videos, CDs and various other items.

Address: http://www.evl.uic.edu/pape/Marx/

## 7. Groucho Marx Slept Here

This site contains a year by year chronology, weblinks, and film information. One of the most unique aspects is an essay about the FBI file on Groucho Marx. There are also wav audio files of Groucho making some of his trademark wisecracks.

Address: http://members.aye.net/~mainman/groucho/

## 8. A Night At The Opera

This is a unique and elaborate site dedicated to the film *A Night At The Opera*. Amongst its features are a section about several scenes from the original script that were never seen. Also over 30 movie stills, and four downloadable full colour movie posters.

Address: http://www.oxford.net/~gmarx/

# The Essential Library

Build up your library with new titles every month

New This Month:

**Laurel & Hardy** (£3.99)       **Marx Brothers** (£3.99)

Film Directors:

**Jane Campion** (£2.99)          **John Carpenter** (£3.99)
**Jackie Chan** (£2.99)           **Joel & Ethan Coen** (£3.99)
**David Cronenberg** (£3.99)      **Terry Gilliam** (£2.99)
**Alfred Hitchcock** (£3.99)      **Krzysztof Kieslowski** (£2.99)
**Stanley Kubrick** (£2.99)       **Sergio Leone** (£3.99)
**David Lynch** (£3.99)           **Brian De Palma** (£2.99)
**Sam Peckinpah** (£2.99)         **Ridley Scott** (£3.99)
**Orson Welles** (£2.99)          **Billy Wilder** (£3.99)
**Woody Allen** (£3.99)           **Steven Spielberg** (£3.99)

Film Genres:

**Film Noir** (£3.99)             **Hong Kong Heroic Bloodshed** (£2.99)
**Horror Films** (£3.99)          **Slasher Movies**(£3.99)
**Spaghetti Westerns** (£3.99)    **Vampire Films** (£2.99)
**Blaxploitation Films** (£3.99)

Film Subjects:

**Steve McQueen** (£2.99)         **Marilyn Monroe** (£3.99)
**The Oscars®** (£3.99)           **Filming On A Microbudget** (£3.99)
**Bruce Lee** (£3.99)

TV:

**Doctor Who** (£3.99)

Literature:

**Cyberpunk** (£3.99)             **Philip K Dick** (£3.99)
**Hitchhiker's Guide** (£3.99)    **Noir Fiction** (£2.99)
**Terry Pratchett** (£3.99)       **Sherlock Holmes** (£3.99)

Ideas:

**Conspiracy Theories** (£3.99)   **Nietzsche** (£3.99)
**Feminism** (£3.99)

History:

**Alchemy & Alchemists** (£3.99)  **The Crusades** (£3.99)

Available at all good bookstores, or send a cheque to: **Pocket Essentials (Dept MB), 18 Coleswood Rd, Harpenden, Herts, AL5 1EQ, UK.** Please make cheques payable to 'Oldcastle Books.' Add 50p postage & packing for each book in the UK and £1 elsewhere.

US customers can send $6.95 plus $1.95 postage & packing for each book to: **Trafalgar Square Publishing, PO Box 257, Howe Hill Road, North Pomfret, Vermont 05053, USA.** e-mail: tsquare@sover.net

Customers worldwide can order online at **www.pocketessentials.com**.